YOU ARE RESPONSIBLE!

by

THE REVEREND GEORGE KING

Published by
THE AETHERIUS PRESS
757 Fulham Road, London S.W.6, England

First Published
MAY 1961

COPYRIGHT OWNED BY
THE REVEREND GEORGE KING

YOU ARE RESPONSIBLE !

Published by

THE AETHERIUS PRESS

By the same Author:

COSMIC VOICE (Editor: George King)

COSMIC VOICE. Volume No. 1

COSMIC VOICE. Volume No. 2

THE PRACTICES OF AETHERIUS

YOUR HIGHER SELF THROUGH YOGA

FLYING SAUCERS

LIFE ON THE PLANETS

THE TWELVE BLESSINGS

THE WISDOM OF THE PLANETS

THE NINE FREEDOMS

DEDICATION

*This book is dedicated to that Great Master
Who prefers His true identity to be hidden by
the name of*

AETHERIUS

ACKNOWLEDGMENT

I wish to express my profound gratitude to the many kind friends who have helped to make this book possible.

PREFACE

THIS is not just another contact story.

The publication of this extra-ordinary volume comes as a lighthouse beacon to a floundering ship, piercing the darkness to say, " Here is safety, here is Hope ".

Shortly after his initial contact with Beings from other Planets and acting upon explicit instructions from the Mystic Great White Brotherhood, the Reverend George King founded The Aetherius Society. He set about a World Mission which was to bring him incredible hardship and suffering. Both he and The Society, were dedicated to the Service of mankind. At first he met determined opposition which waned as he proved his honesty and integrity over and over again.

Beginning with lectures and demonstrating Transmissions to ever growing audiences, the Reverend King soon found it necessary to publish the bi-monthly magazine, " Cosmic Voice ", to carry the Message of the Space People to the swelling number of Aetherius Society Members in dozens of countries throughout the World.

In 1958 a momentous Event occurred, the repercussions of which have yet to be fully appreciated. The Reverend George King served as a Mental Channel for the Master Jesus that He might give His new Teachings —His Cosmic Teachings—to mankind. Thus " The Twelve Blessings " were delivered to the Earth.

At the same time, the Reverend King was appointed the task called, " Operation Starlight ", by which he served as a Channel for Cosmic Energies to be sent into certain mountains that ordinary people might climb to these Holy Places and radiate these Energies out unto the World.

After nine Mountains had been Charged in the British Isles, the Reverend King was directed by a Man from Mars, whom he met physically, to the United States where later he established the American Headquarters of The Aetherius Society in Los Angeles. He toured the country making television and radio appearances and delivering lectures, as well as enabling four of its great mountains to become New Age Power Centres. He has since performed this same Service in Australia and New Zealand. He is presently in the United States again, producing several educational films in The Aetherius Society film unit.

The Reverend George King is the sole Channel for the receipt of information concerning the activities of an immense extra-terrestrial Space-craft referred to as, " Satellite Number 3 ", which periodically orbits this Planet, releasing vibrant Spiritual energies which co-operators on the surface may radiate to all mankind in order to bring about World Peace and Enlightenment.

The reader should bear in mind then, that backing the outstanding metaphysical abilities of the Reverend George King, is an extremely active, religious, non-political, non-profitmaking Organisation, The Aetherius Society, which is serving the Cosmic Plan to bring into being the unification of all mankind in Spiritual Enlightenment.

Service to this Cosmic Plan through such an Organization as The Aetherius Society is the opportunity and privilege of every lifestream upon the Earth.

The Reverend CHARLES E. ABRAHAMSON.

CONTENTS

INTRODUCTION

THE thousands of reports of Flying Saucer sightings which have poured in from every corner of the Earth, during the past few years, constitute the most intriguing mystery of this twentieth century. To the thoughtful man, these thousands of authenticated reports, when studied with open minded care, form what must obviously be the blueprint of an enormous task. The enormity of this task, carried out by hitherto unknown powers, must suggest a necessity which assumes such world-wide implications that we dare not do anything except throw all our efforts towards a better understanding of this vitally important problem. The future of life on Earth, as we know and enjoy it, depends upon that understanding.

How many of us are often prompted by our innermost soul to go forth and explore? How few are willing to undertake the self-sacrifice which this entails?

The Great Teachers of all religions, in all ages, have had to suffer in their unselfish bid to bring true light into the dark ignorance of mankind. These Glorious Few have heeded the inner voice and have gone forward bravely to build signposts to show the way.

Within this book is a message—an essential message—one which is far too important to be kept a secret or revealed only to a chosen few, but must be offered to all. For a way is pointed out for us here—a way we can all tread irrespective of our religion, class or creed. It should be made known that this way is suggested as the only safe one in our age of atomic chaos, by Beings whose vast intelligence and experience put Them thousands of years ahead of the ordinary man. These are the kind of people who are now sending thousands of Space Craft through hundreds of millions of miles of Interplanetary Space in order to turn the tide of humanity away from the great cataclysm it is so surely making for itself.

Let us now be wise before this event: for to be wise after it is to be too late.

PART I.

JOURNEY INTO SPACE.

PART II.

AETHERIUS SPEAKS.

PART I.
JOURNEY INTO SPACE.

CHAPTER I.

THE COMMAND

"Prepare yourself! You are to become the voice of Interplanetary Parliament."

That was the simple and precise Command I received one sunny Saturday morning in May 1954. The crisp tones of the voice which uttered the words, coming as it did from apparently empty space in my little flat in London, brought me to a state of shocked immobility. There was no mistaking the meaning of the message or its importance. Nor was there anything eerie about it, for Sunshine and eeriness do not seem to go together.

I had been a student of Yoga for too long to consider that I was a victim of my own imagination. Yoga teaches the pupil that imagination is an energy which, when controlled, becomes transmuted into a great creative force. Having diligently practised this great science for many years, the reader can be assured that I could not easily fall prey to any flight of uncontrolled imaginative fancy.

How many of us can perform good sailing tactics within a sheltered estuary, yet shiver when the captain says: "Now you are ready to take her out to sea, my lad."

That night, the wonderful opaque curtain which is sleep, could not be drawn across the window of my turbulent thoughts. However, by Sunday morning, the somewhat threadbare carpet seemed little the worse for the extra traffic which frequently passed over it during my nocturnal wanderings.

With dawn came the realisation that, that which cannot be rejected must be accepted. Although I had considered the Command from all possible angles, the one thing I could not do was to reject it. The sages from the East have a profound philosophy which governs the student's acceptance of all their teachings. It is: first, read the theory; second, apply this to the mind; and third, act upon that which is acceptable to the consciousness.

I would like to emphasise that it was not the method by which the Command had been given which disturbed me—the Bible records many such happenings—but the fact that, in order to obey it, I should have to give up another line of metaphysical study just when the answer to an important problem seemed imminent. Moreover, a few valiant helpers who possessed humanitarianism as a common factor, all believed that this answer would be of priceless value to suffering mankind. Indeed, we believed that we were on the verge of discovering a new method of cancer treatment which could cure certain forms of this malignant scourge. Nevertheless, this Command came out of the blue in such a way that no receiver could do anything else but listen and obey.

What use is the most carefully predetermined route on a chart in the face of a violent whirlwind? In this case, a whirlwind produced by the cold, unfeeling march of mathematics into unknown skies—skies from which oft-times rained a killer dust to blot out the benign face of the life-giving Sun. It was soon made clear that a drastic measure was necessary in order to meet a grave emergency. For, after spending many hours discussing an enforced change of direction with my immediate associates without obtaining the type of confirmation required, I retreated into contemplation and meditation.

On the following Sunday evening I was somewhat

startled by the entrance of another man into my rooms. As is the general practice before attempting meditation, I always carefully lock the door. This had not deterred my visitor who, I discovered later from his method of exit, had obviously walked straight through the door. I recognised him immediately as an Indian Swami of world renown. I am not permitted to divulge his name nor much of what passed, but any lingering doubts I harboured, as to whether the intended healing investigation should take second-place to the previous Saturday's happening, were soon dispelled.

My visitor was a great Yogi Adept, who had projected himself in a more subtle state than what is generally known as the physical body; though he looked real enough; even the boards beneath his feet creaked as he crossed the room. To be in His presence was an experience too wonderful to describe, and until now this has been a precious secret locked up with my most cherished memories.

"It is not for you to judge whether you are worthy to be chosen, my son," said this great Swami. He could obviously read my thoughts, and apparently knew that a feeling of personal unworthiness, for what was obviously a large undertaking, had troubled me for days. He had taken a seat facing me and every line of his face and every inch of his spotlessly white robe was perfectly distinct to me. Even the chair had creaked slightly as he sat down. I had often read about feats performed by the Masters of the East, who could project themselves for thousands of miles in a flash, and appear as life-like as if they had just alighted from an aeroplane. But this was the first time I had ever witnessed such a feat performed by someone whom I knew to be very much alive.

His voice was gentle but had a peculiar penetrating property. "The real necessities of the present age," he

declared, "brought about by the unfeeling march of
science into the realms of the atom on the one hand,
and the wrong thought and action of the masses on the
other hand, can only be met by those few who are ready
to tune into the emanations now being sent on to this
Earth and become the servants of the Cosmic Masters.
You are only one of many called upon to prepare yourself for the coming conflict between the materialistic
scientist, who has arrived at his conclusions by the cold
application of mathematics and the occult scientist who
has arrived at his conclusions through the recognition
that God is all. Pray, be still, meditate and open the doors
of your heart and mind to the precious waters of Truth."

After saying these things, my instructor gave me
further Initiation into a certain Yogi exercise, the
careful practice of which brings about an ability to
travel from the physical body in such a way that full
memory of all the experiences gained are retained by
the traveller. He also stated that those people best
fitted to form a group of willing helpers would be
brought into my orbit. I was informed that I should
receive a letter from a school of Yoga in London, which
I should attend for some months and that I should
diligently practise the exercises taught there.

The Swami, having imparted this information, bowed
with the politeness of a race which enjoyed an advanced
culture when ancient Britons still painted themselves
with woad. Then he made his exit by walking straight
through my locked door. I dashed to open it immediately, but the long corridor outside was deserted. My
friend from the East had disappeared.

This was the spur to action. As it was necessary to
set up a group to help in the coming campaign, I gave
this formation all my spare time attention. This was to
be a specialised group of workers who would be willing

to devote hours of their valuable leisure time to help one person to produce the goods. They had to have full belief in the somewhat mysterious project and at the same time be knowledgeable in the basic aspects of occult and contemplative practice. On the face of it, even as few as half a dozen such people would be difficult to meet, but the task seemed to work itself out. In fact, I was able to describe these people a full week before I met them for the first time.

Meanwhile I was invited to a school of Yoga in London by a letter which came out of the blue. The hours spent in the exercises and prana-yama (a system whereby the universal life force is controlled through deep breathing and breath control) yielded good results. Quite soon after the deliverance of the Command, I was able to tune in and receive telepathically, information which was relayed over millions of miles of etheric space. A message from Venus was recorded on our tape recorder for the first time.

CHAPTER II

YOGA AND TELEPATHY

The purpose of this book is to show the reason behind the frequent visits of Flying Saucers to Earth. I do not attempt a treatise on occult practice, but a few words of explanation as to why telepathy can be brought about by the science of Yoga will not be amiss.

The word "telepathy" means communication between mind and mind other than through the known channels of the senses: in other words the training of a mind to tune into, receive, and translate into speech, thought waves which are relayed by another mind. If you take a cheap wireless set into your drawing room and switch it on, you may receive two different stations. If, however, you exchange it for an ultra-sensitive set, you can tune into a score of stations one after the other. The room is the same in either case, so that the difference in reception is not produced by positioning; but by a sensitivity incorporated into the design of the better set by the makers.

Now the brain of man is a delicately balanced molecular mechanism capable of receiving and transmitting "mind stuff" which travels through the ether. This "mind stuff" is all permeating and as will be seen later: "Wherever there is ether there is mind." Indeed, we are a certain number of atoms floating in a vast sea of ether and mind. It can easily be seen, then, that a sensitive brain can attract, slow down and bring about a translation into sound (speech) different aspects of this vast

24

sea of mind which surrounds everything in the whole system. In a much simpler way, your wireless receiver picks up a relayed signal, which travels through the space between the atoms of gas in the atmosphere—the space known as the ether—and causes it to produce its original sound through a loud speaker. Thoughts are waves of primary electro-magnetic energy, and because energy can be radiated out into space in all directions at the same time, so can these thought waves similarly be transmitted.

After being brought into intimate contact with a human mental process, "mind stuff" must be changed in some way from its pre-reception state. The energies released by this change form, for us, a product which may be called—understanding.

No one can deal with the complications of mental function in a few words, but it is necessary here that a reader, unfamiliar with such subjects, should have a working idea which will help him to appreciate more fully the matter contained later in the book and how it was made possible to receive such information.

The reception of mind by the brain is one aspect of its function: the other aspect is transmission. Most mental transmission is carried on through automatic translation into sound, when the electro-magnetic impulses radiating from the brain operate upon the vocal chords. Hence the human race evolved speech (language) as the main medium through which ideas could be exchanged.

Everything in the world is in a state of vibration or movement and the difference between a rock and a tree is really that each vibrates in a different way. So it is with mind, otherwise we would all think the same things at the same time. The different sensitivities of man's mental receiving apparatus causes him to attract different mind waves, or degrees of mind. If this operates in one way, so also must it operate in reverse. Action and reaction are opposite and equal. This is a metaphysical law which, up to now, has never been disproved. Therefore, if a brain is capable of reception, that same brain is also capable of transmission of thoughts. These thoughts can be tuned into, picked up, understood and translated by any brain capable of sensitive attunement without employing the recognised senses. This is telepathy.

After establishing the fact that telepathy is possible, the next step is to put the theory into practice. The science of Yoga is one sure way of doing this.

It is a fact, now accepted by the medical profession of most forward countries, that brain function can be enhanced by deep breathing. The Yogis, after thousands of years of study, have not only proved that controlled breathing brings about controlled thinking, but that it creates an ability to concentrate for great lengths of time upon any selected object, be it a fish, or the mind emanations relayed by a Being from another Planet. The basic principles are the same and any difference is one of degree only.

Breath is life. Your life span is a certain number of breaths. The most important reason for correct breathing is not the absorption of extra oxygen and nitrogen by the body, vital as this is, but the feeding of the nervous and mental system by—prana. Now prana is the name given to the universal life force which provides us with the energy necessary to function throughout the whole range of movement. This applies to the higher bodies as well — the etheric, astral and mental bodies of man. Without prana, no mobility of any kind would be possible on a psychic, mental or physical plane. Prana is an all permeating vitality providing every atom with that energy which makes internal movement of the particles possible.

Prana is contained in all the water we drink and all the food we eat — yet chemical classification is not possible, for it is an energy contained within the particles of matter constituting these things. Hence the most important reason for drinking plenty of clean, fresh, sparkling water and eating the correct foods is apparent. But the fully enlightened Yogi Masters discovered that the greatest supply of prana and that which is most easily accessible to man, was contained in the air he breathed. Also, that certain breathing methods would put those who diligently practised them in tune with this universal supply. These methods energise the nervous centres and brain to such an extent that they bring into active manifestation certain latent faculties which can be controlled by the will. The vital pranic energy can be consciously directed into each of the six major nerve centres of the body, thus activating the chakras in the subtler bodies. These chakras are centres which become veritable miniature Suns in the etheric bodies of those who constantly recharge their whole vehicle with vibrating pranic energy.

Those occult students who know the science of breath are on the verge of Adeptship. All the latent Spiritual faculties are brought into usable realisation by correct application of these natural laws. The most wonderful sight on Earth is to see, through the eyes of clairvoyance, the internal pulsating and rhythmic ebb and flow of the mighty forces vibrating within the heart and Christ centres of one who is really an Adept. To be in the Presence of such a One as this, is to be filled with His wonderful radiations. For these centres, when correctly opened and functioning as God intended them to function, become veritable beacons of vitality which flood everything that comes near to them with the very essence of Life itself. No words can possibly describe the wondrous beauty, the magnificent blending and interplay of the most delicate colours of the subtle forces which whirl at unimaginable velocities within the chakras of the Masters. Indeed, only one clairvoyant sight of these magnificent pools of God's light is necessary to know why the Orientals called them after the loveliest flower on earth — the lotus.

Through these chakras enter the mind forces, which travel to the brain. They resemble little flood gates which, when fully opened, can accommodate a great flow from the sea of "mind stuff" which surrounds everything. In addition to taking in energy and mind from outside, some of these vortices of force also radiate magnetic energy outwards from within. The majority of successful "faith healers" have the solar plexus chakra working well and are able to radiate their pranic magnetism outwards and into the corresponding centres of their patients, thus invigorating them and in many cases, bringing about a cure which would be called miraculous by the uninitiated. Often this is done unconsciously by the healer.

The balance of these chakras depends upon many factors. Karma generated in previous lives does inhibit or help the correct workings of these subtle centres, as also does the flow of prana throughout the nervous system, especially through the spinal column. For, although the chakras actually exist in the subtle bodies of man, they have their neuro-physical counterparts in nerve ganglia which branch off the spinal column, rather like branches growing out from a tree trunk.

Correct, controlled breathing can bring about a conscious control of the pranic energy contained in the breath. When this has been accomplished, through careful and diligent practice, then the chakras can be vitalised in such a way as to bring into activation certain psychic faculties which have hitherto been dormant. The student then becomes very sensitive and among other things, can tune into the mind emanations from another being. His little "flood gates" can be opened at will and in pours this "mind stuff".

I found that the best results were obtained by first practising certain prana-yama exercises, after which a positive trance condition was consciously brought about by very deep concentration upon a certain chakra. If telepathy is done in this way, then you may be unaware of what you are saying at the time, depending upon the depth of trance you are able to induce. This, of course, must not be confused with the negative trance condition which is brought about in some séance rooms. Such a condition is caused by the medium so negating his mental faculties as to allow a discarnate entity to make use of them. Such so-called mediums do not know who is going to use them, for how long, or even, if this dangerous condition is practised often, when such a trance condition will appear. I have the greatest respect for those mediums who are able, at will, to tune into mental and Spiritual radiations emanating from great beings inhabiting spheres of a higher vibratory octave and different dimensional framework from the one in which they exist, but I feel it is very essential to warn all those who seek to develop the negative types of trance condition not to do so. These misdirected people can only tune into the astral realms and may contact, or be used by, a being less evolved than themselves. All mediumship has its pitfalls, but if a would-be medium studied the teachings of the Masters and acted upon their advice, then little harm could result.

This aspect of Ancient Wisdom was practised until it

was possible for me to tune in directly to the mental emanations of a being from Venus who, with his permission, we agreed should be called — Aetherius. This name was chosen because of a deep occult significance which cannot be revealed at this stage. Those who know the underlying reason for this action will appreciate the need for secrecy. I would like to point out, however, that to be mysterious for its own sake is the procedure of an adolescent, but that there are things which can only be revealed when very special conditions prevail. For this reason it has been decided that the actual deep breathing exercises which were instrumental in enhancing those psychic powers I had already developed to some extent, should not be revealed in this book.

The Yogis say that when the student is ready, the Master always appears. Any occultist worthy of the name, has proved this to be perfectly correct. If you lead a thirsty horse to the water you do not have to make him drink, nature will do that. So with man. If he is thirsty enough for wisdom he will knock hard and often upon his inner door until it is "opened unto him". Meditation is the key to the door of ALL knowledge, whether it be the details of the propulsion units of a Flying Saucer, or why some potatoes have more eyes than others.

By learning and applying these simple, though not necessarily easy, Ancient practices, it became possible to translate the thoughts of a Member of the Interplanetary Parliament and to speak them, so that all who were interested enough could hear their wisdom——wisdom evolved through aeons of time which had been well tried in the fires of adversity and not found wanting in any way.

The discriminating reader will soon notice that this wisdom, coming from a Master, now living on a Planet far more evolved than Earth, is fully applicable to all of us. The Master Aetherius does not claim any originality for these teachings. In fact he says: "Originality is not possible. It was all here in the beginning." But in these teachings are the deepest occult truths put in a simple way for everyone to read, understand and then act upon. A simple rendering of such deep concepts proves one thing quite conclusively—that whosoever could bring this translation about, fully understands the major things which have puzzled the ordinary man for aeons of time. At great cost to himself, this enlightened Being, The Master Aetherius, has given us a priceless key to the cupboard in which is hidden the blueprint of behaviour which will lead the World out of the chaos and muddle into which we have steered it.

When I say "we"—I mean that most of us are responsible for the present state of affairs now prevalent upon this "dark little island". How nice to sit back in the scented harbour of our own procrastinations and put the blame on other countries, governments, even the man next door. It will not do! The time has come for every man and woman capable of human feelings of decency, to reach out a hand and accept that responsibility which they have for too long passed on to others. The responsibility of loving their neighbour *more* than themselves!

I have been to Mars and Venus in a state of consciousness which far excels my ordinary state and know that whatever comes from these sources is beyond question. This has been made possible in order that the experience could be shared in a simple and understandable way with everyone. My dear friends, please believe me when I say that such unforgettable experiences as the trips to Mars and Venus can be undertaken by any would-be space traveller if he only opens his heart and mind to the God which dwells in the "Kingdom of Heaven which is within". Why put your faith in a chariot, or a lumbering great rocket ship, when you already have the finest space vehicle in the whole Galactic System awaiting your command?

May I be forgiven for repeating the instructions given by my Indian Visitor, recorded in the first Chapter— "Pray, be still, meditate and open the doors of your heart and mind to the precious waters of Truth."

CHAPTER III

MY VISIT TO VENUS

"Greater things than I have done, ye will do if ye believe in me." So said the Avatar from Venus some two thousand years ago.

Great things we can do if we believe in the power within ourselves at this moment. Power just awaiting the right procedure in order to put it into active manifestation—a procedure which is given to every man when he is ready to receive it. All things, even travel to the Planets, are possible to the wise. The only true democracy is wisdom, for wisdom is knowledge activated by power through love. The result is freedom. No longer is the Planet you live upon a prison, but a place offering scope for exploration which would satisfy the most adventurous soul.

Interplanetary travel is not a mere futuristic pipe dream: it is a practical possibility to all those who are willing to sacrifice some so-called luxuries of civilisation and exert sufficient effort in order to bring it about. Why wait until science has made a lumbering monstrosity driven by pure brute force, which will have to attain a speed of 25,200 miles per hour in order to escape from the gravitational pull of Earth? Already you have at your command, a vessel capable of attaining the speed of light, driven by the subtle forces of thought, which will cover the Earth–Mars distance in seconds.

If ever there was a wise statement which is in every way usable and practical, it is: "Seek and ye shall find." This is a fact which each of us can prove to be workable, even in this day of pseudo-civilisation. In every aspect of its meaning, this philosophical concept is provable to all who are willing to exert the required effort in order to find that which they seek, be it a way to reach Venus in 1961, or a means to cure cancer without using a radio-active cobalt isotope which is liable to destroy good tissue. Fixed concentration upon an objective will reveal the way of attainment. But there must be a brave positive approach and an un-wavering belief in the possibility of attainment. Establish these fundamental essentials and eventually the necessary procedure will be revealed in such a way as to make attainment a living, existing experience.

When I was fifteen, I knew that one day I would visit other Worlds. Twenty years later, I left my physical body in a little room in London's teeming West End and travelled in an orbit around Venus. It shone beneath me like a huge diamond — a mist-covered diamond which was brilliantly illuminated by a great light from within. I did not try to land the first time, being completely satisfied to describe an orbit about two thousand miles outside of its dense, misty-looking atmospheric belt. I feel sure that, if the average reader believes me, he will appreciate the warm, inner joy which I felt for a week after this first orbit around another Planet.

Next, I was instructed by certain occult sources to try to reach the Moon when it was full. If ever the phases of the moon seemed to stand still, they did that month. That celestial crescent simply would not grow, as it had done before, into a full circle of cold light. But at long last patience reaped its just reward. For there it was, a full, round, benign face beaming down invitingly. There was I glued to Earth, for try as I might, I could not bring about the division of bodies which makes projection possible. The whole book of advanced prana-yama was thrown into my efforts, but without success. The same thing happened the next night. After the fourth attempt had failed I drew the sword of faith, life's greatest protector and carefully whet this upon my innermost soul, in deep contemplation of desire and motive.

For my fifth attempt a different procedure was adopted.

I decided to creep up on what was left of the visible part of the moon, for a stratagem was obviously the order of the day. I practised Yogic breathing exercises with the utmost care, to gain mental control and enhance magnetic potential. When the crucial moment arrived, I flung myself out of the physical envelope and in less than a second was hovering over my mother's bed some miles away . . .!

Now positive projection such as this enables one to leave the material body in a state of superconscious awareness. All one's powers are much enhanced in this state, including the powers of perception. Thus, by using this extra-sensory perception, I could see my mother's heart was not as steady as it should be. It took perhaps three minutes to put this right — then the Moon.

The speeds attained by that envelope of consciousness which leaves the physical during directed projection, are incredible, although often no sensation of velocity is experienced, probably because the actual travel takes place in — and becomes part of — a higher aspect of the space time continuum. The phenomenon has an existence in at least a seven-dimensional continuum which seems to blend together the facets of time into a whole. In this respect such a phenomenon has experience of the ever present Now. One can remember living through a change, yet be unaware of the time element measuring that change. When you become an Adept at predetermined projection, after the division has taken place you can, in a flash, be aware of surroundings millions of miles away. It is only when you concentrate upon these surroundings that you become conscious of actual movement.

I floated a few feet above the surface of the Moon. To my higher state of consciousness, the Moon seemed to be surrounded by a magnetic sea of ever-changing colours. These changes had a certain pattern which denoted the activation of a magnetic field of subtle order. The fluctuation of these stupendous and colourful Lunar magnetic "tides", was a sight of pure fascination, yet one which I seemed, for some reason, to understand at the time. To put that reason down on paper, however, is another matter, for one's conscious mind is really absurdly ignorant—as all "projectionists" have no doubt already discovered.

I was not surprised to see the beautiful geometric design of the space station. This was built of a "plastic" substance which reflected the ultra-violet cosmic bombardment which continuously rained down and penetrated the surface crust of the Moon. Above the domes of this camp, slowly revolving to follow the path of the Sun, was a concave-shaped mirror with a conical aerial of gold coloured metal extending from its centre. This metal glowed as though it was lighted from within. I believe the whole mirror was made out of prisms of a substance which must have had a melting point way above that of glass. The parabolic mirror was obviously revolving on the top of the power house, which I tried, unsuccessfully, to enter. There was some kind of magnetic force screen around the whole dome which resisted all attempts to enter.

I was to learn later that this space station, built

by the Venusians and Martians, had been specially protected to stop anyone or anything from entry until permission had been gained from the proper quarter. The reason for this is now quite obvious to me. Within that power house must be the secrets of vast natural forces which, if wrongly used, would cause great destruction. Many such things have been seen since the contact with The Master Aetherius for this projection was undertaken just prior to actual telepathic contact with Interplanetary Parliament.

After returning to the body, I made it clear to my group that when Earth men visited the Moon, they would see proof that others had been there before them. A week or so later confirmation of this was received from a scientific organisation in California. I understand they used hypnotism to cause one of their investigators to project to the Moon. However, this investigator returned with news of a space station. As there had been no previous correspondence between us, this was considered to be a very interesting confirmation of my findings.

The second visit to Venus ended in much the same way as the first, namely, in a description of an orbit around the brightly glowing Planet. Landing was impossible because of the barrier of repulsion which enveloped the whole Planet and its atmospheric belt. These people must be thousands of years our seniors in the sciences of applied magnetic fields, otherwise they could not bring about such a gigantic coverage. To seal up this Planet and its atmosphere in a magnetic envelope, must necessitate a manipulation of colossal natural forces, not to mention an exact knowledge of the physics of these forces. We all need to thank Holy God that these beings come in peace, for, if they were as warlike as we, they could obviously knock this puny ignorant little Earth of ours out of the System as easily as a man can brush a fly from the back of his hand. I fully realised, for the first time and in a way which can never be erased from my memory, the stupendous power and knowledge possessed by the people I had been commissioned to contact.

In all practical occultism such as this, a bravery factor is essential. I had been told some years before, by an Initiate from Thibet, that this factor was inherent within me. But even so, that night's experience taught me that discretion is, beyond doubt, the better part of valour. I decided not to try to visit Venus again until permission had been granted. Not that I had been hurt by a third party in any way, but if a blind man is suddenly cured and sees the Sun for the first time shining in all its golden glory, that experience teaches him more about it than ever he knew before. He may have previously learned much about the Sun from others, but all his painstaking study would not reveal as much as that first, full-sighted glimpse of the real thing. A modern, high velocity rifle is a little boy's plaything until it is loaded—only then can its real power be demonstrated.

Some little time after the telepathic contact with The Master Aetherius had been made, I was granted permission to visit the Planet Venus. Details of preparation were precisely and personally given to me, with a request for strict secrecy until after my return to Earth. I was told that I would be expected at midnight, on the eighth of July 1954. May I assure my readers that what follows next is a completely true account of the happenings on Venus, set down immediately upon my return to Earth.

I visit the Valley of the Sun—on Venus.

From the balcony of the Temple of Solace, I looked over the wonderful purple valley to the yellowish cloud-wreathed mountains beyond. My guide, "Patana", sent out a scintillating rainbow-coloured magnetic ray, which very gently explored my mind. When I expressed a mental wish to follow him, I just floated on this wonderful ray, down from the great heights into the valley below, coming immediately before a marvellous construction which appeared to be a Temple. This was topped by a gigantic dome, which shone with such a blinding light that all its colour emanations seemed, in some miraculous way, to blend together into a living white.

I was informed, through the guiding ray, which acted as a channel for telepathic communication between "Patana" and me, that this Temple was the Spiritual Centre of Venus. High Spiritual radiations from here penetrated into every human mind on Venus. I was not allowed to go nearer than a mile, or so it seemed, from this Temple of Brilliance, but from that distance a terrific shock was experienced, even through the glassy bluish screen which "Patana" materialised around me, by thought, as a protective measure.

I gazed enraptured at the tall spires and great towers; some of which were triangular in shape and position, topped by this mighty translucent dome which I knew to be throbbing with life.

My thoughts were swept back through my past on Earth—then forward into the mists of future, like dry sand grains in a great whirlwind. Here was an unbelievable Power, above the dimensions of consciousness, time and space, as we know them.

The physical body of "Patana" melted away and He became like a huge bubble which changed through every colour—colours which defy description, but a bright purple and a pale rose pink seemed somewhat predominant. Great ripples of colour swept over his large vaguely transparent bubble-like body from the top downwards. As these moving colours swept past the middle of his egg-shaped body they would change in a subtle manner, becoming slightly darker. Meanwhile, another colour would pervade the fine bubble-like structure at the top and this colour too, would sweep downwards, darkening as it did so, causing his whole shape to vibrate rapidly.

I heard a strange little trilling sound, which seemed to come from within myself—a whispering note which started high and soft becoming louder and deeper in tone as each colour darkened. It sounded rather like a wailing, but one of supreme ecstasy. Colour and sound were a united experience and "Patana" was one with that experience. I feel that only the actual experience of such Divine bliss would give one a complete knowledge of it. My conscious description of this superconscious perception is totally inadequate.

Even though I was contained within a force screen of protection, I felt such Power, that something akin to awe thrilled every essence of that part of my being which had been projected to Venus.

I stood before the gateway to Eternity!

It was as though EVERYTHING were there.

A supreme, pulsating, scintillating, living brilliance which knew me more completely than I had ever known myself. Subtle, gentle, not coarse enough to be openly persuasive: yet with a Power that seemed nothing short of Macrocosmic. A giant of giants, with the sweet gentleness of a child. I have no idea what would have been felt in the direct rays from the Temple. I wanted, with all my heart, to reach out some mental hand and imprison Time within my grasp, that I might stay there forever.

We were back on the exquisitely carved crystal balcony of the Temple of Solace. "Patana" had now rematerialised himself a body of more familiar shape. He told me that from this Temple in the Valley of the Sun came the outpourings of the Supreme Logos of the Planet Venus.

That the Masters of Venus, Who came from Saturn, could relay this Power unto Their students in a degree determined by their readiness to absorb it. In this way the complete experiences demanded by birth on Venus could have their full expression.

A little room, a green meditative light, a ticking clock . . . I was back again. Oh my dear friends on Earth, I swear to you that this experience was worth all the previous hours of effort which I had expended, in order to bring it about.

How can I enjoy reading tomorrow's newspapers after this—?

CHAPTER IV

THE MARS STORY

The first time I thought I visited Mars, I was nearly killed! Although, since I have inhabited a physical body in the present incarnation, there have been many occasions when my habitation has been nearly brought to an abrupt halt, this was the nearest I have ever been to death. It was probably my own fault for not carefully cross-checking the request to visit Mars which came to me from an occult source. At the time, my intuitional feeling intimated that this request should be obeyed, but later I realised that more information should have been gained before the attempt was made. I do not put this forward as an excuse, of course, for even an idiot can be wise after the event!

To those readers who would say that the following account is a piece of imaginative science fiction, let me counter at once with the trite rejoinder: "Truth is stranger than fiction." Indeed, I have myself often read stories that have made me wonder whether they have really been true or whether they have been written as fiction in order to get them into print. Some of them, if narrated as truth, would surely be scoffed at.

The Master Aetherius says that there is no such thing as pure fiction, because everything must contain an element of truth. If you dwell upon this statement you will gradually realise the depth of hidden meaning within these words.

It should also be noted that, if one lies deliberately, one will never gain wisdom. This is the Law. Take to truth and you will be able to discriminate between that which is true and that which is false. As a man who has now devoted his life, even to the extent of sacrificing a very well paid position to search for truth, I would be foolish to indulge in a fictional phantasy with a true-story label on it.

Those enlightened beings who now govern my major moves, have advised against revealing all the facts behind the Mars Story. However, I feel that the revelations I can make should not only prove interesting to the open-minded person, but also show how an ordinary individual like myself can contact the Love and Power of God and use such assets in a very practical way.

I left my body on Earth, in accordance with my usual custom and came to a halt on what was thought, at the time, to be one of the two little moons which circle Mars. I came before a building made of silvery metal resembling aluminium. I knew, however, that here the comparison ended, for aluminium could never withstand the incessant bombardment of cosmic rays which must be prevalent in such a place unprotected by an envelope of atmosphere. In a flash a quick tour of outside inspection was made. The building was perfectly rectangular in shape, looking like a huge metal box standing on its side. In one of the narrow ends was an opening through which I entered.

The interior was not unlike the inside of a bank vault, except that the walls glowed with a bluish radiance which seemed to come from within the metal itself rather than resemble a reflection such as would result from a light in the room. In front of me was a small, stage-like platform backed by a large oblong of opaque grey material, not unlike the type of plastic I had seen previously in some walls of the space station on the Moon. This oblong shape was about 12 feet in height by 60 feet in length. To the left hand side of this oblong, between the outside metal wall of the building and the plastic shape itself, was a small square black patch. It looked like an opening into a dark room beyond.

It was not until I got to within a few feet of the strange looking platform that things began to happen. Then they took place so quickly that no words of mine can do justice to their spontaneity. In what seems now, to the slow conscious mind, a millionth part of a second, my life was weighed in the balance of existence and the Lords of Karma decided in favour of its continuance . . .!

When I came to within a few feet of the platform, I was stopped dead in my tracks, for the dull, greyish-looking screen behind had suddenly sprung into life. Its colour changed in a flash to a vivid blood red, as though some giant but invisible hand had reached out and torn away a covering from its smooth surface. This flood of intense red light seemed to struggle to penetrate my whole etheric structure. I knew beyond doubt that my presence had been detected. In the same instant a dwarf figure appeared in the black opening, raised a weapon and fired point blank at me without appearing to take any sort of aim. It was as though I had been unmolested until my exploration had brought me to a chosen spot and then the screen had been suddenly switched on and the dwarf had fired at me instantaneously. There was no time lag whatever between the two occurrences. It was similar to a flash-light camera in which the shutter operates simultaneously with the flash-bulb.

As previously stated, during this type of projection one possesses a super-conscious awareness and abilities which, when suddenly flung into high gear, can react in a manner which the ordinary mind would regard as impossible.

A thin blue deadly ray came hurtling towards me with

the speed of light. Although, in my present state, I was
capable of moving with incredible speed, this stood me
in no stead, for the opening behind may have been automatically sealed to coincide with the other two happenings. To try an escape through the floor or walls was not
the answer, for I did not know the full properties of the
material of which they were constructed. I had seen intricate force screens at work before and for all I knew
such a magnetic process may have been in operation
within those walls. That, at any rate, could have
caused the bluish glow I noticed upon my entry.

The last defensive weapon that would occur to the
ordinary conscious mental process was the first to occur
to me then, tottering as I was on the brink of death,
caught like a fly in a web spun by some nightmarish
spider who had stepped from the pages of futuristic
science to prey upon the unsuspecting present. My only
method of defence was *thought* and I used it in its most
concentrated form. I flung out my thoughts at four million
times the speed of light, to meet that deadly ray. The
invisible fingers of the thought form, highly concentrated
by the motive of self-preservation, reached out and took
hold of the end of the ray nearest to me and spun it into
a spiral. This spiral curled around itself like a whirlwind
of light. In an instant it stretched, like a huge oval bobbin
of snaking blue cotton, up to the roof where it tore a great
hole through the metal. Through this aperture I made a
rapid escape. Hardly had this been accomplished, however, when a bright bluish green flash marked the short
circuiting of some type of electro-magnetic field.

Those occultists who have passed from the kinder-
garten of theory into the senior school of practice, know
the terrible dangers of projection, and accept them. This
experience had its physical repercussions, but happily
they were soon completely cleared up by my good friends,

some of whom are excellent Spiritual healers. At such a time as this, I cannot stress too highly the importance of good Spiritual healing, coupled with the self-induced healing of Yoga. In fact, after many years of study and practice of all aspects of Spiritual and magnetic healing, I feel sure that this is the system of medicine of the future. So-called miracles can be brought about by these methods, more especially if the patient, adopting a cheerful outlook and positively affirming success, co-operates fully with the healer.

Mars again: but this time I travelled there in the chariot of caution, although I could not accept the fact that Mars was really hostile to an Earth traveller. My previous astro-navigational calculations had obviously gone wrong, but if I had not been on Mars or one of its moons on my last visit, then where had I been? I had not left the Solar system. The fact that there was, within our little Planetary system, an evil as low as that previously contacted, had troubled me so intensely that the question had to be answered—and dealt with. The continued safety of Earth may depend upon this.

I landed in the desert of Mars between two of the great longitudinal vegetation belts, some scientists still call them canals, which stretch from pole to pole. The floor of this desert was red-brown in colour, though not made up of sand as we know it, but of a much finer substance almost like eroded top soil, caused no doubt by baking in the Sun and through lack of water. It was a desert of dry, reddish-brown dust which was radio-active, but not in the degree to hurt my etheric counterpart.

I felt a tremendous pull towards a distant vegetation strip lying due East of my present position—a pull which was exerted by some outside source rather than by my own curiosity. I allowed myself to be drawn steadily eastwards in that thin atmosphere under the purple

sky of Mars. But every faculty was alert, for once again
it was obvious to me that my landing had been detected.
This time, however, I was fully prepared for any hostile
action shown by the inhabitants. About five miles away
from the long strip of giant vegetation, I stopped and
prepared my magic in the shape of a thought form.
This was projected ahead as a forward scout. The
thought form was manufactured in such a way as to
"assess" the mind emanations from any contacts and
relay this assessment back to me. In this way, if escape
became necessary, I should have a good start. Such
a process is used by black and white magicians alike—
but with entirely different motives, of course. My motive
was defensive not offensive and I had decided to run
rather than cause harm to any humanoid life form.
This decision was not the result of fear, but to comply
with the Law. St. John said, "One has to be as wise as a
serpent—but as harmless as a dove!" That is the Law—
God's Law I had made up my mind to abide by it.

I had found that all powers seemed greatly enhanced
by the existing magnetic conditions on Mars. This meant
only one thing—that the inhabitants of the Planet had
used their prevailing magnetic conditions to such an
extent that these conditions were now amenable to meet
all stresses imposed upon them from any source.

The projected thought form entered a smallish dome-
shaped building, made of a bright green coloured plastic
type material and travelled into a circle of Martian
people. Through the psychic link which joined me with
my thought form, it was possible to detect a strange
atmosphere. The strangeness was not caused by the
mental vibrations emanating from people existing on a
Planet which was foreign to me; rather was it as though
their thoughts were placid upon the surface but turbulent
beneath. There was trouble here—serious trouble. Here

were people—nice people—suffering acutely; though not in the ordinary way, but as one could imagine a kind man would suffer if forced to witness the cruelty of others. It seemed that the whole Planet was in terrible danger and that it was my duty to help if at all possible. The impending cloak of caution was discarded and I entered the green building and absorbed the thought form back into my psychic bodies.

One stage above the earthly mental plane, language is no longer a barrier. For upon the higher psychic and intuitional planes mental information is not reduced to sound as in speech, but is relayed within a certain vibratory framework which is universally understandable. I stood there, a foreigner from a Planet about fifty million miles away, yet I could easily understand that group. Moreover I was visible to them, although I could have sat in an ordinary drawing-room all night on my native Planet and unless a good clairvoyant was present, remain coldly undetected. Truth is indeed stanger than so-called fiction.

This was a meeting of the General Assembly of Mars. They had met to discuss a terrible danger which threatened the Planet. They were fully aware of my previous visit to the Holy Shrine on Venus and had requested my presence because of that. It was easy to understand now the terrific pull towards the red-brown Planet.

It seemed that about a month before, a gigantic meteorite had been arrested as it passed within 400,000 miles of Mars. The scientists had measured its atomic weight as one thousand times that of hydrogen. Accordingly they had sent their robots on to this planetoid to commence mining operations for a geological survey. All work of this kind is done by remotely controlled robots which, I found later, were very complicated pieces of mechanism almost human like in their ability if not in their appearance. Excavations had progressed well for a short time and a Spaceship had brought first samples of ore to the laboratories on Mars. These samples were placed in specially prepared containers because of their intense radio-activity which was much above any-thing the Martians had discovered up to that time. When the next shipment of ore was ready to be collected, a Martian freighter put out to pick it up. As the trip was considered to be only a short routine flight, a young Captain was detailed to make it. Because this was his first Command after some years of rigorous training, his vessel was kept under close surveillance by the observa-tory. Just as he had vacated the gravitational pull of Mars and was in free fall, a little over an hour's travel away from his objective, all radio contact with the mine was suddenly cut off. There were two engineers in the mine on the foreign planetoid who were directing the robots in their excavational duties. The powerful radio from Mars could get no reply from the mine. The young Captain was immediately informed of this strange silence but he decided to continue his journey and investigate. After all, no organic life had been discovered on a large lump of cold jet black rock, the orbit of which was strictly under Martian control. However, when the freighter was within one hundred thousand miles of its objective, tragedy occurred. The Martian observers saw what appeared to them to be a huge purple cloud rush towards the vessel and engulf it for a split second, after which it disintegrated!

Latest type Space-ships were immediately sent to investigate, but their magnets only pulled in tiny pieces of metal dust—all that remained of what had been a large Space freighter over 3,000 yards in length. The Captain and crew of six had all perished. One of the small, fast interceptor ships described an orbit nearer to the meteorite to investigate. It perished in the same way!

There followed an immediate recall of the fleet to Mars, because a large projectile had been detected by their radio screens. Three great men will have their names for ever enshrined in the archives of bravery, for they caught up with the projectile and having no weapon on their ship, they rammed it, head-on. I learned later that their vessel had been a saucer-shaped scout ship loaned by Venus, which was not armed. The collision caused a huge atomic explosion which the Martians described as of No. 10 intensity. It is interesting to note that our present H-Bomb is considered to be a thermo-nuclear weapon capable of etheric distortion of No. 4 intensity. Had this projectile landed on Mars, or Earth, only God knows the destruction it would have caused.

To complicate matters further, the supposedly dead planetoid had developed a motion of its own outside of the orbit originally determined by the Martian scientists. Two conclusions had been deduced from these startling happenings. One was that this planetoid was inhabited by a form of intelligence not hitherto known of. The other was that this intelligence had learned to gain control of the robots sent there for mining operations and had computed into their electronic brains the knowledge and ability to manufacture advanced atomic weapons and use them.

I was told, in answer to my thoughts on the problem, that it was now realised, in the light of experiments carried out on the sample delivered previously, that because of the extreme atomic instability of this heavy rock, if any weapon of a magnetic nature was brought to bear on it, this would cause atomic chain reaction, he resultant energetic release of which could easily destroy the two Martian moons. This would cause

irreparable damage to the Planet Itself as well as to the
Earth. So that was the problem. An intelligence from
deep space, with no finer instincts, was installed in a
fortress which, if destroyed, would wipe out its destroyer.

"What about an appeal to other Planets for help?" I
asked.

"This is our problem. It would appear that a force has
been released which has caused the rapid and grossly
mutated growth of a form of life unknown to us up to the
present. We have disturbed something hitherto dormant
and the resultant responsibility can be laid at our doors.
What we cause we must right—and soon. We know that
we have what you would call one week in which to right
it. We, on Mars, as you on your Planet, are directly
responsible to the Lords of Karma for our deeds. The
pattern imprinted upon the timeless Ether by the ritual
of all our actions remains, until transmuted by its
creator."

"If you cannot ask a higher power for help without
interfering with your Karmic responsibilities, then if
you ask a lower power to help and together you succeed,
then you have virtually helped that power to advance,"
I thought quickly, and before the Leader could raise any
objection, I proceeded to relate my previous experiences
when supposedly on one of the Martian moons. "So you
see I, too, have been caught up in this web of
conditions."

After listening intently to my experiences, the Leader
told me that it was obvious that I had landed on the
planetoid in question.

I pushed my claim, as though entranced in the grip of
some deeply felt duty. "As I have been there and failed
in some mission destined by the Lords of Karma, it is I
who must return."

The Leader of the group was surrounded by some

type of protective screen which turned colour from green to blue as he lapsed into meditative silence. He looked very beautiful as he sat there breathing deeply. He looked, to my psychic sight, like a large-chested human covered with this most delicate wispy substance which enhanced his handsome features so greatly. I discovered later that he had been a deep space Captain and had learned how to generate this protection at will.

"I must accept your offer. I will tune into you at"—a rapid calculation took place here on a complicated piece of machinery—"8.30 on Tuesday next, in your Earth time."

There were occasions during the next week when I almost wished the promise to return, as arranged, had not been made. Somewhere there was an answer to this problem—but where? Mars had long-range magnetic rays capable of the disintegration of mass. So had our common enemy. We knew, by what had happened to the freighter, that the "thing" on the satellite had a terrible weapon which was effective and uncannily accurate up to a range of one hundred thousand miles. This would be used, whereas the Martians could not employ such a weapon in retaliation, even if they wished to do so. A few fast neutrons, together no bigger than a millionth of a centimetre, were capable of starting an atomic fire worse than ten thousand Hydrogen bombs exploded simultaneously. Not a pleasant thought, especially if you study what Aetherius has to say about the disastrous effects caused by thermo-nuclear fission.

This was my first problem in Interplanetary military strategy and it gave me a worse headache than if I had imbibed a quart of whisky and port wine.

The knowledge, deep down within me, that I had accepted a grave responsibility, acted as a nightmarish spur which goaded me ever onwards. The fact that there were others in the Planetary system who could easily supply the answer to this problem, was not the point. The science of medicine has reached its present position because a few brave men have taken upon themselves the responsibilities of finding cures for terrible ailments. When the going became unbearably tough, these pioneers did not sit back and wait for their successors to discover what they had failed to find. They burned the midnight oil—so that their lamps could be put out with the rising Sun which shed its pink glow upon success.

A verse of poetry which I learned at school kept strumming through my mind:

"But it's not for the sake of a ribboned coat,
Or the selfish hope of a season's fame,
But his Captain's hand on his shoulder smote,
Play up! Play up! And play the game."

I did learn one great lesson here, namely, that when faced with a problem such as this, it is no use relying on mental deductions brought about by the conscious part of the mind. The thing to do is to give all the facts, as you know them, to that vast store of previous knowledge, the subconscious and be open-minded enough to allow yourself to be guided into the correct path. I have always known intuitively, that the subconscious mind of a mouse knows more about natural function than the conscious mind of the greatest Earth biologist. Also, that there is a direct mental link between the so-called subconscious and intuition. As previously stated, in my case, Yoga was used to enhance this mental link. But the key which opens the door to success is contemplation and meditation. Deep meditation will guide one to any and every answer to any and every problem. The result of meditation is the energy released by the explosion of forces on the intuitive, or highest mental level. This is the way to release and to bring into active manifestation, the tremendous powers lying dormant in mankind at this present moment. The Great Masters have proved the point for us time and time again in the most practical of ways.

It was on the following Sunday evening, or most probably very early Monday morning, that I found the answer to this complex Space problem. I discovered it in a book which had been lent to me by a practical occultist of great experience. At the time, I must add, he knew nothing of my dilemma. Indeed does God act through others to help those who are stranded upon the path, providing their motives are high enough. After almost a week of hard concentration and frustration there it was, all laid out for me in black and white. Spoken by no less a personage than The Master Jesus Himself to an audience of a hundred people in Thibet in 1900 A.D. There was one way and one way only of ridding Mars from His terrible visitor and this was it. The answer was so obvious and so simple that it had up to now eluded my somewhat frantic search. I was childish enough to dance around my room, for I was filled with such joy. My neighbours must have thought me quite mad. I wanted to tell someone—anyone—all about it. But the disadvantage of living alone is that there is no one to tell—save any invisible discarnate entities who may be floating around at that time. To tell these would be superfluous, however, for they can read thoughts anyway.

Tuesday evening, a ticking clock, a blue green light, deep breath—darkness which comes with closed eyes, haze turning from grey to blue, swirling colours spinning and spinning, the sickening feeling in the pit of the stomach, the clock fades from audibility, a light getting brighter—the thunder caused by the forces whirling around in the vortex of tremendous energy which is the Christ Centre—centre of all movement, a thousand colours getting nearer and nearer—now surrounding consciousness—one moment tottering on the brink of bodily inhabitation—then glorious freedom.

Such are the experiences of projection. What is whole man if not the image of God?

I did not land on Mars, but was guided into a Venusian saucer-shaped vessel lying about a quarter of a million miles from our adversary. This Saucer was controlled by a being from Venus who commanded a crew of five Martians and myself. It was the job of the Flying Saucer to become a mobile target and thereby attract fire from the small planetoid. In this way an analysis of the kinds of projectors used against us could be made. Also our presence would keep the enemy fully occupied while long range radio X-ray soundings were made by a larger Martian vessel in order to ascertain the position of the factory where the robots were manufacturing weapons for their cruel master. The reason why a Venusian craft was used for this purpose will cause many followers of the famous Dr. Einstein to snort in disgust. However, let me say that less than a century ago some experts "knew" that man could never travel faster than 30 miles per hour!

The Venusian Flying Saucer was chosen because of its ability, in free space, to exceed the speed of light! We had a force screen around the outside of the vessel which would take the first shock of a direct hit. This gave the operator a precious split second to accelerate up to a speed just over the velocity of light and thereby out-distance the deadly ray which would lag behind. Or, in other instances, a direct hit would be made on our "shade", which would travel behind us when we were actually exceeding the velocity of light much in the same way as the sound wave follows a jet plane which has broken through the sound barrier.

As soon as I arrived on this Flying Saucer, which was at least 120 feet in diameter, I was instructed to project a mental vision of the exact procedure which was going to be personally adopted in order to deal with the mutated intelligence from outer Space. My thoughts were instantly reduced to a vast number of colours for most of which Earth has no name. These were projected upon a tiny screen, somewhat similar to a cathode ray tube used in modern television. From the narrow end of this tapering tube a strong beam of light shone forth. This was made up of the "thought colours", which whirled around so quickly that they formed a beam of a single bright colour. The beam passed through another piece of apparatus which concentrated it still further until it appeared as a mere pin prick of the most intense light I have ever seen. As I looked at the light caused by my own thought pattern, my admiration for the brilliance of the science of these people was more firmly cemented than ever before. A Martian busied himself with some very intricate and no doubt extremely delicately balanced instruments through which mental potency, in its entirety, could be accurately calculated. I was being carefully weighed again, but this time in a kind but nevertheless just balance. Judging by the expression on the analyst's face, the answer was none too good.

I knew that in a short time from now I was going to be landed on that cold metallic planetoid and left there alone with a job to do which must be carried out successfully. Failure meant something too horrible to contemplate. To Mars it could mean great catastrophe—to me—well only God knows what happens to one whose etheric body is destroyed. I was not able to dwell on these negative thoughts for long because we began to move towards our objective. The 250,000-mile gap which divided us from our waiting enemy began to close at a tremendous rate.

When only about 50,000 miles separated us, the projectors from the satellite came into action. Two long beams of light reached up towards us like the thin clawing fingers of some evil giant trying to pluck a worrying bird from the skies. The little Flying Saucer literally jumped from her even course when these beams contacted her envelope of force which acted as a temporary screen of protection. The whole world outside turned into a swirling mass of purple as the atoms of the screen were excited by the collision between the two opposing energies. The rays thrown up at us were of two different vibrational frequencies; one just above ultra-violet and the other just below infra-red. When these were short circuited through any mass between them, their efforts to join one another again through that mass caused such a violent agitation that the atoms which made up the molecules of that mass were flung apart. Hence the disintegration of the Martian freighter which had not been protected by any magnetic force screen.

In much less time than it takes to relate, a beam of violet light from the Flying Saucer cut a way out of the now useless force screen, like a hot coal would burn its way through a thin paper bag. In a split second our velocity was put up to 200,000 miles per second and we were soon over a quarter of a million miles away out of range of those probing fingers of devilish destruction. Again and again we dived, swooped and turned, sometimes at right angles, within range of those projectors. Each time we adopted the same procedure—that of discarding our burning force screen, reforming another one and swooping in once more. Here was a harmless sparrow worrying a deadly cobra. The terrific speed and manoeuvrability

of that Flying Saucer is something I shall never forget.
Never once did the Venusian operator move. He looked
like an incandescent egg suspended about a foot from
the floor, for he had discarded his physical body as soon
as the action began. His physical body, in a state of semi-
dematerialisation, looked like a little grey cloud. It was
fastened in a locker by a system of magnets. I loved him
for the Master that he undoubtedly was. It is interesting
to note that these people are such Masters of the force
of gravity that, although the Martian crew were in
physical bodies, their flesh and bones were not damaged
at all by manoeuvres which theoretically should have
crushed them and the Flying Saucer into pulp. Even
though there was only a very mild gravitational pull on
the ship from the outside, it must be remembered that
at times we were reaching the speed of light.

While we were thus attracting the attention of the
robot soldiers on the planetoid, a Martian vessel had
been able to get in close enough to take radio X-ray
soundings from which could be ascertained the position
of the main concentration of armament. The factory
where the robots were remanufacturing themselves was
also pin-pointed. These robots were acting automatically
with mathematical precision on the information relayed to them by the controlling entity.

Two large Martian vessels swooped in to the attack
simultaneously. A flash of green fire from the belly of one
of them denoted the use of some kind of weapon. This
green flame snaked *slowly* through space and hit the
black floating rock beneath, forming an ever-spreading
green blob over a portion of its jagged surface. I was
interested to know exactly what this was and was about
to shape a mental question when I was jerked to an
abrupt, startled halt.

After the attack, one of the Martian ships turned

quickly and retreated, but the other went straight on down towards its objective. It was within a few thousand miles when a red and blue ray came snaking up and hit it squarely in the middle. Instantaneously, a great purple cloud seemed to form around it. A second later there was nothing left of it save a faint bluish glow in the cold void of space. One hundred and sixty one Martians had deliberately sacrificed their lives so that their comrades could use their weapon and escape to safety. They were all immediately released from their physical bodies to travel onwards to places where, because God is Love, they would reap a just reward for their selfless sacrifice. At least, this was my interpretation of the incident at the time.

Far away in the distance a colossal magnetic storm was raging and spreading over an area of several million square miles of hitherto changeless space. This was the result of the electro-magnetic perturbations caused by the release of tremendous energy through the projectors of our adversary. As though that were not sufficient, the planetoid began heading straight down towards Mars Himself, gathering momentum with every split second. The entity controlling it, apparantly intended to crash on Mars or its force screen knowing that tremendous damage would result from the nuclear explosion as this piece of rock approximately the size of the British Isles disintegrated.

I was filled with apprehension. I turned towards our Commander. The Master from Venus had gone! There was a low soft hum coming from the secondary propulsion unit of the Flying Saucer. This was broken suddenly by a staccato, rasping noise which made even my etheric flesh creep. Through the single eye which poured forth a beam of soft multi-coloured light from the middle of my forehead, I took in the terrible picture projected on the screen of the machine capable of assessing and measuring the qualities of mind emanations. The screen showed a black smudge. This was the emanation coming from the mental apparatus of a foul entity now intent on wiping out the Planet Mars and presumably Earth.

"Even from Terra," said the Martian operator, in thought; "We have never seen the like of that. Your Earth Masters throw a blue, violet, or sometimes yellowish-white image upon that screen. The collective mental radiations from your large cities form a grey picture flecked with sparks of blue and yellow. *But never have we seen a perfectly black one until now!*"

I was filled with anxiety for our safety. "What are you going to do about that thing. It will not take long to reach your world at its present speed?"

The Martian nodded his head towards the empty space where the Commander had been. "Our friend will return. He has gone to Saturn for help."

"But Saturn is millions of miles away. They . . ."

My thoughts were abruptly cut short for I then saw one of the most beautiful sights in the whole Planetary System. Why I deserved to be allowed to gaze upon it for even a moment I do not know. It was a Space vessel from Saturn! It slid silently into psychic vision—a huge, perfectly round sphere of glorious radiant light. The atmosphere inside the Martian Flying Saucer was filled with an indescribable fragrance. Delicate, sweet, almost tantalising in its pure freshness, this perfume permeated the whole of my psychic structure and I was at once filled with a new life. I was watching a modern Star of Bethlehem which The Master Aetherius later referred to. No wonder the Wise Men of the East years ago followed their bright star. Indeed they would have been lacking in wisdom had they not done so. One glance at that glorious sphere of scintillating loveliness caused my confidence to well back in a great flood. Even now, when recalling to mind that vision of perfection, I drop my pen and say, with childlike humility, "Thank you God, for creating the Lords of Saturn!"

Hundreds of thousands of miles away, little pin pricks of light appeared as the Interplanetary Space Fleet arrived. Against the backcloth of dark purple space they looked like hundreds of tiny glow worms. Yet each one was a vessel, the product of a science thousands of years ahead of Earth. They darted to and fro, some singly, some in formation the shape of an age-old mystical symbol, as they began their work of negating the great spatial magnetic storm which was raging. No longer was the cold ether of Interplanetary Space a lonely void; now it was filled with the different life forms of a full half-dozen Planets, working in complete unison like some great silent machinery handled by the Gods Themselves. Forty million miles away, on little Earth, men, made tiny by the limitations they put upon themselves, sucked their pipes and declared that humanoid life on other Planets was an impossibility.

The deadly radio-active satellite had now increased its velocity and was being guided straight towards Mars.

"We can only spare you five seconds on that, after which our action will be dictated by the Great Ones."

This mental instruction came from my Martian companions. Something seemed to tighten up inside me, a strange quiver of fear passed through my whole body. What could I hope to do in five seconds against that colossus of intelligence, the possessor of powers of black magic the like of which even Mars had never met before?

The great sphere from Saturn gave birth to a tiny glowing bubble-like object, then disappeared before my eyes as though swallowed up by some gigantic but invisible monster. The shining bubble drifted towards us, described a tight orbit around the almost stationary Flying Saucer and the next moment I was inside it staring at the Commander from Venus. We moved rapidly towards the objective.

From a few hundred feet away, it looked really weird. A large black piece of rugged rock the size of the British Isles, half covered by a bright green blob. This green patch was a plastic glue which had been propelled there by the Martian attacker in order to seal off the robots and make their weapons useless. This was quite a feat, considering that it covered an area of hundreds of square miles and had been accomplished with a single dive on the target under heavy ray fire. The Martians killed just before this glue substance took effect had not died in vain. It looked like a gigantic piece of coal over which some unworldly artist had spilt a huge paint pot.

I looked around the spherical bubble, which had now come to a halt, for some sign of propelling machinery but none was visible. I looked at the Venusian, floating about a foot from the bottom surface of the space bubble, glowing like a large oval incandescent egg. Then I looked back at the cold black uninviting mass beneath. I felt like a swimmer who had regarded the high diving board from a deck chair at the edge of the pool and thought the dive an easy one, until he had mounted the ladder and stood on the edge of the pitching springboard and had seen the tiny pool yards beneath himself.

I turned again towards my companion from Venus. His shape had completely changed! He now appeared in an Earth body of wonderful stature and brilliant radiance. I recognised him and gasped in astonishment. For though there are no photographs of this Radiant Being on Earth, recognition was simple. His countenance was the complete personification of brotherly beneficence.

He spoke six words unto me. Just six simple little words; yet they gave me such unbounded power that I stepped fearlessly through the side of the bubble and landed on the planetoid.

"The Love of God Never Fails." This was my only weapon.

It came gently, almost imperceptibly at first, that eerie voice—yet it was not a physical voice, nor even a thought, but something akin to each—groping. Then it went, leaving me only conscious that it had been. Then it came again—trespassing—feeling its way into my mind, like some filthy tendril of a blind climbing monster groping for a foothold. Again the sea of blackness retreated—leaving me with a feeling of revulsion at the contamination caused by its presence. It came back—this time with some horrible renewed vigour, exploring the dark caves of my mind and stirring up the black slime which had lain at the bottom of the stagnant pool of forgetfulness for countless centuries.

"The Love of God Never Fails."

The exploring mental tendrils curled away as though hurt by the Light. But again the mental waves of that black sea broke upon the shores of my mind with a psychic stench which was putrefying. I remained quite still and let these black waters break over me. When they were withdrawn into the trough again, I visualised a white light growing stronger and stronger. The whole ground beneath me quivered violently. Some great prehistoric animal was trying to shake a worrying bird from its broad back. This time, the mental waves were warm, gentle, fawning. I began to pray.

Then came promise. A promise of great power. A promise of power which could rule whole worlds for a lifetime stretching far into the future. Of riches beyond my wildest imagination. A promise of delights—all delights.

I was shocked, for not even in my basest imaginations had I realised such things were possible. These pleasures were to last for ever and ever.

"How Can God's Love Fail?"

The whispering voice told me I was alone, unprotected. I visualised the Master whose presence I had just left.

The whole planetoid trembled and shook violently from end to end. This was my last chance and I took it. As God is my judge I forged from the matter of Love a Golden Sceptre of vital power. My whole etheric structure, acting as a channel, trembled as the Golden radiance surged forth. I no longer stood there alone—the whole Host was around. No longer did the time glass measure change—for all became unchangeable. Save one, which cringed and coaxed, threatened and swore. This evil entity from the very depths of hell itself split the planetoid in two with a blinding flash of searing flame. Yet we stood in silence and loved in silence. The greatest things beneath Heaven are performed in silence. The Sun rises and sets in silence. The Moon moves mighty oceans with a power which operates in silence man's body, a great tree, a tiny blade of grass all grow in silence. A great galaxy of stars moves with tremendous velocity through the silent ether—in silence. The most eloquent voice is—silence. I stood in silence before the profundity of all silent eternity. For silence is Reality because it is unchangeable. Love, the mightiest power in all creation, operates in the depths of absolute silence. So I flung all my powers of meditation upon the Great Silent God within.

That thing, which only a short time ago had threatened the safety of the Planet, Mars, recognised its coming defeat. For Love was the one weapon which it could not conquer.

Real Love, not the physical thing that Earth men call love, if resisted, instantaneously multiplies the power of itself by four.

The entity must have known that if it accepted the power of this love it would be changed as a result of such voluntary acceptance. If it resisted, then would the power go on multiplying itself until shattered resistance was finally broken down.

I would like to point out that this happens only if the feeling of pure selfless love is held absolutely steadfast above all else. This was the teaching of The Master Jesus which I had read earlier; the teaching upon which I had staked my very salvation.

The entity which had created a cleft stick was now being held by one. There was no way out of its dilemma. The end was guaranteed by the beginning. Only when the spark of consciousness vacated that vile, shapeless, black mass which it had inhabited, was the Silence broken. Then did the silent voice, which is the voice of Silence, utter its Great Decree.

"Thou Art That!" it said—and was silent.

So passed outwards, onwards and upwards, the life of the mutation which had come from far away out of deep mysterious space. From the depths of its own prison of cruel darkness, it passed through the portals to teaching, light and finally—freedom.

Back on the Flying Saucer, with my etheric body cleansed of contamination, I watched the two pieces of that radio-active planetoid being towed away by the vessels from Jupiter to some safe place in the System.

The Great Master who asked me to relate this true story exactly how it happened, save for those omissions which He considers should not yet be revealed, has done so because it has a moral and is a lesson for all mankind— whether they be contemplating the exploration of the vastness of Interplanetary Space or the mysteries of atomic space.

I learned later that this planetoid had been specially prepared by the four evil dictators who rule a world called by pseudonym "Garouche", which is situated at the opposite side of the Galaxy from our Solar System. This evil weapon was actually launched against Earth rather than Mars. The Martians knew this and arrested it, sacrificing their lives so that no damage would come to Earth which could not have protected itself against such a force.

The real reason I was allowed to intervene was because I was living on Earth. The evil entities who had made this weapon wanted to conquer Earth because, as they are water dwellers themselves, the conditions here could be easily adapted for their use. The idea of these monsters was to kill all humanoid life on Earth and then inhabit the seas which cover a greater part of the surface. In this way they would have a base at each end of this Galaxy. They worked out a brilliant stratagem, that of incorporating an intelligence into the rock formations of the planetoid so that if it was ever interfered with it had a tremendous natural weapon within its own rock like body so to speak—that of atomic radiation which it could control and direct. It therefore concluded that it could not be destroyed by any weapon outside of itself without causing terrible havoc.

The real reason behind the sacrifice of life made by 174 Martians who died in this Interplanetary Operation to save mankind upon Earth from destruction has now been revealed. This is one of the truly staggering aspects of the story which I have omitted in accordance with instructions from Higher Authority.

Although my etheric body was cleansed when I arrived back on the Flying Saucer after the conflict, my physical body, even though it never left Earth, being as it is, dense reflection of the aura, sustained a severe injury which no healing can ever put right. The majority of men suffer as a result of their own Karma—*the small minority suffer even worse as a result of the total Karma of the Earth.*

So ends the Mars story. With the Eastern rising Sun has come all the wisdom—with the Western setting Sun must come the practical application of that wisdom. For we stand now upon the threshold of a new age, during which thinking man must consciously vacate the wrong paths of his near ancestors and stride boldly down the straight, narrow way as a brave explorer of the future.

May I now, with a humble gladness in my heart, introduce you to a Master from the Interplanetary System, Whom we have called—Aetherius.

PART II

AETHERIUS SPEAKS

CHAPTER V

LET US HELP YOU

THE MASTER AETHERIUS

"I have been given to understand that you would like me to speak on some simple generalities.

"I am an Interplanetary Liaison Officer and a Representative of the Planetary Government. As such it is my mission to spread our message of Peace to certain factors upon Terra. Now, Terra is one of the few remaining Planets not yet accepted into the Central Interplanetary Government.

"My dear friends, I would like to go out of my way to tell you that we have great feeling towards you on Terra and we know that certain of you, have a commendable approach to the more Divine concepts of everlasting existence. To such people, I would like to say that I realise your difficulties, in the midst of existing pseudoscience, as certain scientists are trying to make their own laws. Some people recognise that it is essential to cooperate with natural laws and it is to these people that I come. It is to these people that many of us have come in the past and many more will come in the future.

"Many Flying Saucers, as you call them, have landed on Terra and the operators have talked to the Masters in different countries. Now we are branching afield a little more and are willing to meet certain *specialised individuals* in order to give our message of goodwill.

"A certain amount of literature has been written about us, and it has been noted that through this literature runs

71

a streak of fear, which has been put in by the writers, in order to make it more sensational.

"Disregard this, so far as we are concerned! We are Beings more evolved than yourselves. We have indeed outgrown your Earth and have gone on to a higher plane of material existence, so you can see that, should we do you any harm, we would be guilty of a grievous crime.

"It is my job, as one of the many Governmental Representatives, to counteract the wave of fear that has swept through some of your terrestrial minds. We know that, as a man has no feeling towards a spider, because it is a different shape and lives in a different way from the way he does, some of you will have no real feeling towards us, unless we prove to you that we are only too willing, not only to approach you in Peace, but to help you out of your present difficulties.

"If you will only let us, we can help you in your meteorological difficulties, thereby cutting down the death rate caused by aircraft crashing when they fly through certain clouds which contain currents of air sometimes travelling at over one hundred miles per hour.

"We can help you by teaching you how you can irrigate and cultivate your deserts, so that they can again become as fertile as they were when the Great Pyramids were built. We can teach you how to grow such crops as to make famine appear like one of the atrocities of the dark ages. In fact, if you will let us, we can advise you how to make things so different, that within fifty years, the earlier half of the century will seem like part of the dark ages. We cannot trespass upon those grounds which are closed to us. The choice is yours—you can receive us with open arms and we will help you to the best of our ability—or you can reject us.

"We trust that certain of your political factors will not be overcome by their own pseudo-importance and so reject the hand of friendship that is now being offered.

"We can help you in your primitive educational system, so that every one of your pupils is given that experience demanded by his Karma.

"We can help you in your hospitals, so that your system of medicine will be able to say that cancer, tuberculosis and venereal diseases are things of the past. If you want us to help you, stretch out your hands to us.

"We can help you in your geological surveys, so that earthquakes, such as the recent ones in the small islands of Greece, could never happen again. This is worth taking into consideration, because we have discovered vast movements of land masses at the bottom of the Pacific Ocean, which will bring about dangerous conditions in the near future.

"We can give you an agricultural system twenty five thousand times better than your present one if you take down your notice—'thou shalt not trespass'.

"Now, I hope that I have given you some little idea of why we are surveying your Planet. To us, you are a people in desperate need of advice. We are willing to give you this advice, if you will let us: if you want it—if you will use it in the right way.

"So, my dear friends, the next time, and it should not be very long from now, that you see a strange object you call a Flying Saucer, in the sky, remember that, if it is manned, it is manned by people living in physical bodies, as you live in physical bodies. Remember that it is manned by people who, sooner or later, will land on Earth to hold out to you the hand of friendship and offer you help and advice; by people who want to see Terra fully represented in the Interplanetary Parliament, and learning from the people of Mars and Venus, Neptune, Jupiter and Saturn. These people want to see Terra, not a place of famine and distress, of war, strife and disease,

but a place where men worship at the shrine of the Holy
Logos, as they do."

CHAPTER VI

EDUCATION ON VENUS

THE MASTER AETHERIUS

"WHEN the Cosmic Masters came to Venus from Saturn, we welcomed them, and they built for us a crystal temple exactly in that position where we could contact the Supreme Logos of the Planet. We have been using these Spiritual emanations ever since. We incorporate the emanations coming from the Supreme Logos of Venus into our daily lives and especially into our educational systems.

"We also use symbolism in education and we have found that the shape you call the triangle is indeed one of the most important shapes in the Planetary system at the present time. So we arrange our classes like this: we have the Master sitting at the head, his leading pupil forms the apex of the triangle; two more pupils form the base of that triangle. Now these pupils are carefully picked out by what you call metaphysical analysis, brought about by the Master. He determines which pupil is ready to receive certain information, taking into consideration the Karma which has been brought into being by that particular pupil in former existences. If the Master sees that a pupil needs a particular experience in order to bring about a required result, he takes hold of the mind of that pupil and transports it to any place in the Cosmic System which will afford the exact experience necessary for the pupil's evolution.

"So we have the Master passing on information to the most advanced pupils first, and they in turn will pass on information to pupils less advanced than themselves. It is rather like water passing through certain sieves. Let us suppose the water contains chemical elements of certain consistency, the larger pieces of these elements containing the greatest power and the smaller pieces containing power which has been tuned down. First of all you have your really advanced pupil, who will take out the large pieces and the other pieces gradually pass through the filters, which in this case are the minds of your pupils, until at the end the last pupil takes out the very small pieces of element, or the less profound parts of Truth.

"In this way we have no inhibitions caused by useless rules, set up by people who do not fully know why they make these rules. This happens in your educational system. In our system, the Master, at His own discretion, brings about a full expression and realisation of those conditions and experiences which are pre-determined by his pupils' behaviour in former existences.

"On Venus we do not ever eat meat; we have evolved past that stage. We live on Solar energy direct. Some of our younger ones eat and drink the juice from certain berries and the juice which is given off by certain trees, but apart from that, the tremendous emanations radiating from the great temple in the Valley of the Sun afford our sustenance. It is only a matter, you know, of raising your particular vibrations to a state where the molecules of the body themselves no longer need coarse food, but can assimilate the higher vibrations given out by the Sun. I understand that your sages, since pre-Atlantean times, have been able to illustrate this point to you. I might say, in deference to these sages, that indeed we cannot give you on Terra any more knowledge than your great Teachers have already given to you. All we can do is to present the Ancient teachings in a more modern dress.

"Does anybody wish me to elucidate at all, on any point I have raised?"

Question:

"I would like to ask one question, if I may, on the difference between the old and new ways of putting forward the Ancient teachings. Do I take it that scientific apparatus was not used in former times and that perhaps methods of symbolism and ritual were so used to gain the same effect? Would you elaborate a little more and tell us whether nowadays we should combine the two, or concentrate upon 'new dress' ways of doing these things?"

The Master Aetherius:

"The most sensitive apparatus in the world is the human body. That was used instead of using a machine made of coarser matter. Sensations which stimulated certain nerves in such a way as to bring about a definable result were noted by the Ancients and catalogued. It was known that there was nothing on Terra which was as sensitive as a nerve membrane.

"The surest way, indeed the quickest way, of bringing about mento-physical sensitivity, which will translate and make understandable the higher aspects of Truth, is to raise the vibrations of the body and the brain by constant meditation upon the highest possible concept. You can bring about results in the way I have just mentioned thousands of years before the same results can be brought about by pseudo-scientific means. The real scientist, in our humble estimation, is the man who makes a temple of his body—a temple in which he can work in perfect harmony and study and understand the great natural Law within and outside himself."

CHAPTER VII

INTERPLANETARY POLICY

THE MASTER AETHERIUS

"I would like to say a little more about our political system, although the word 'political' has to us, as you will see, a very different meaning than it has to you.

"Now then, I am afraid your terrestrial political system is one of the standing jokes on Mars and Venus. It would appear that your politicians have stated many times in the past that religion and politics do not mix. This is a very unfortunate statement and indeed one which is quite wrong. In order to form water we have two gases; in order to have a correct political system we have two major philosophies which, amalgamated together, become one.

"No political system is at all complete without a religious foundation.

"How can you have water from oxygen alone? You must have the hydrogen to combine with the oxygen in order to have water. You people on Terra vote for and keep a political system in its place which is not in any way complete.

"Our religion is a simple one, which has been built upon the foundation that God is ALL.

"God, as Absolute, is the One Cosmic Simple.

"There cannot be anything else outside of this original cause.

"This original cause, of course, must contain even a political system which you adopt on Terra, but if you consciously strove to put the correct philosophy in the

78

correct place, you would have a system that would not produce the world calamity and chaos and even internal chaos that your present system produces.

"On Venus we elect Representatives to go to the Interplanetary Parliament, the major seat of which is on Saturn. These Representatives are elected by the Ancient Ones, who have vast knowledge. They elect only those people who have lived through experiences which put them, by natural law, on to a higher plane of existence.

"The Representatives are often chosen before their birth and if necessary are called into bodies by the Ancient Ones. They are then prepared so that they will be able to put forward all aspects of the Truth. They are able to see the *four sides of a rectangle* and are able to reach agreements with their fellow men, a lot of whom inhabit bodies of a vastly different shape than they may do. This not only applies to the Planetary system but also includes major factors in the Milky Way.

"Our Representatives travel to various places, some of which are younger—evolutionarily younger—than we are, then they help the inhabitants to gain the experience which they see is necessary to them.

"I am a Representative of Venus in Interplanetary Parliament, and as such I have taken upon myself the duty of speaking to people upon Terra through this Mental Channel to make them think in a different way so that they may be brought out of the mental rut into which they have fallen. This reorientation of thought will bring about a heightened awareness and rise of all consciousness and when the time is ripe the right men from Terra can be chosen to go to the Interplanetary Parliament. I use the word 'Parliament' for want of a better word.

"Before a man is chosen as a Representative, he spends much time in the presence of the Ancient Ones, who give him the highest teachings that he is able to assimilate. He is capable of the same metaphysical feats that your greatest Masters are capable of. He must be capable of instantaneous mental projection from his Planet to any other Planet in the Parliamentary system, so that he may be able to converse with other factors and understand their point of view. He must realise and must feel that even if he has to make a great sacrifice, himself, for the Truth, this he must do without the slightest hesitation. All selfishness is washed away from such a one, because he could not be selfish and go through the initiations demanded by such a position. There is no question as to whether he is fit to be a Representative, this does not arise. Because the Ancient Ones have great wisdom they can see that he is able to perform his task properly. The people who are younger upon the Planets have full confidence in the judgment of the Ancient Ones, because they know that this has been proven throughout the ages. The judgment of the Ancient Ones has been tested in all the fires of adversity and it still remains like a new metal without stain or oxidation.

"There does not exist on any of the more advanced Planets a monetary system; it is totally unnecessary. Everyone has exactly what he needs to have.

"One of your Masters, two thousand years ago, said that man should have that which he needs. This is the basis of our economic system. Every man, woman, child, animal, plant, metal, even the very ground upon the more advanced Planets, has help, because the ground itself, rocks themselves, have to have certain experiences. These rocks are helped to gain the experience which is demanded by their past Karma.

"All is mind, of course, all is knowledge.

"In these conditions a monetary system is totally unnecessary and because of this wars and strifes do not arise.

Of course, we have our problems, but they are mostly created by young Planets such as Terra and others which are situated outside of the Solar System.

"Please note—even some of the Suns I refer to as Planets, because if I use the word Sun, terrestrials immediately think of something which has an interior temperature of 40 million degrees and is totally unapproachable, which of course is not so. Even some which do have an interior temperature of 40 million degrees are just as pleasant to inhabit as Venus—in a different body, of course.

"These younger Planets create most of our problems which we solve to the best of our ability. Just as we have offered to help you, our job is to solve the problems of those people who need us. The very fact that they have problems proves that they need certain help.

"It is obvious, of course, that the actual work of salvation must be undertaken by each individual, personally. But there has been an allowance made in the Divine Law for you to be guided in this vital respect.

"The Master Jesus was resident on Venus and the Lord Krishna and Buddha, Sankaracharya, the Master Satsat and Fortsat—the last two you may not have heard of as they work very quietly—were Interplanetary Beings who came to give you help. This was not outside the Divine Plan but was contained within it. In other words, you have been helped to overcome your difficulties. Your own Karma which you have built up for yourself over previous generations has to be adjusted by you, but it is not governed by such a cold heartless law as you think. It has mercy within it.

"That mercy is shown by the fact that you have had great Masters upon Terra in the past, that you will surely have another Master in the future to advise you, to help you, to flood the world with His Spiritual vibrations, to throw light into the darkest corners of your own ignorance. These things are a living proof that there is mercy, there is love, there is hope, even for the most base of all life.

"We are approaching you slowly, gently, subtly, but surely. If you go out and tell people that you have heard a telepathic broadcast from a Member of the Interplanetary Parliament and that Being stressed the fact that He comes with love and has offered practical help, that will do very much good. You see, a lot of your scientists have gained certain information about us in a very vague mathematical kind of a way. But it is not your scientists that we are relying upon, it is you. It is your mystics, your occultists, your press, your writers, we are relying upon. Make no doubt about this, in the near future you will notice a great swing take place in your press. Those very people, who, a few months ago, would have laughed at any mention of communication from Interplanetary Intelligences will change their opinions. These are the people, these are the sources, we are using. We are using very many more sources which cannot be divulged at the present moment. Have faith and courage and you will not regret it.

"The time will come when your reward will be great peace and joy.

"Let your mathematicians play about with their three-dimensional formulas; you stick to your six-dimensional beliefs and have your nine-dimensional faith and you will see the twenty five-dimensional power work out. Does that help you?"

Question:

"Can you please tell us if the recent hurricanes in America and other places are in any way due to atomic explosive experiments?"

The Master Aetherius:

"Some time ago I told you people that if you went on as you were, you would bring great hurricanes down upon yourselves. Please believe that we have done as much as possible to help you in this respect. We have intervened with our implosive mechanism and have absorbed a lot of the 'static' radio-activity which has dangerous radiations. As a result we have prevented *some* meteorological calamities but unfortunately we have not been able to prevent them all. To prevent them all would have meant that you people would have had to change your thoughts and your actions. You are the moulders of the world! I have said this before; you mould the world like one of your great Masters moulded wood at one time. All of you are responsible for the hurricanes and the droughts and the famines. The natural law is perfect and because it is, it must react in a certain way to a certain cause. Your wrong thinking and action is the cause. Certainly, my friends, your atomic explosions together with the wrong thought and actions of your world are responsible for the recent hurricanes. I warned you people that these things were going to happen. I would have been very happy had I been wrong."

Question:

"Suppose atomic experimentation was stopped, then how do we protect ourselves in case of war?"

The Master Aetherius:

"Now two sides are needed to fight a war; not only one side—two. When the mob seized The Master Jesus, one of His followers, whom I have spoken to many times since, attacked a soldier with a sword and the Master told him how wrong he was to attack him with a sword. It takes two sides to cause a war. If you people, this moment could have a hundred per cent faith in Truth,

Light and Love, you could easily throw away all your weapons. You would still stand victors of the world and nothing could hurt you, nothing could ever destroy you. England is one of the chosen Spiritual centres of the world, believe it or not. Nothing will destroy that: such has been declared by the Ancient Ones, it will be so and nothing can alter that. Therefore you could easily dispense with all your foolish nuclear toothpicks and still be victors of the universe, make no doubt about it. If this were not so, then all your Masters were fools and we know they were not.

"Because some countries are ruled by force, that alone will guarantee their downfall. They will not be rulers of the world, they will not dictate, for long, to the world.

"Because it takes two sides to cause a war, I am advising you to destroy your weapons now, believe in God and have faith and you will rule the universe. This military might will soon fall to the bottom of the ocean—and I really mean that.

"If you believe in the Truth you cannot possibly be conquered by anything or anyone. One man, can guarantee, *guarantee*, the freedom of this or any other country, it matters not whether he is killed or chopped to pieces.

"As I have previously stated, our leaders, unlike yours, are willing to suffer in the way that I have suffered, not for their own Planet, but for other Planets which they are trying hard to help. Your Earth leaders are hardly willing to suffer one blow to their false pride, so you have subterfuge, you have this cold war, this blaze of politics, this false glory. That is the downfall of Terra. Until you get back to the simple teachings of your own Masters, you will never do any good.

"You have to get back to these eventually, so why not make a start now, yourself?

"When you do this, your world will seem different to you. It will not appear to be against you—but you will be able to see the glorious Spiritual Light within it.

"Remember this, there is one sure way to destroy communism. You can rid your Earth forever of this by making conditions so good that no one will ever want it. *That is the only sure way.*"

Question:

"How old are you?"

The Master Aetherius:

"3,456 Earth years. I am only a young man, very young. It has been very nice speaking to you. Good-night."

CHAPTER VIII

THE DANGER OF THE H-BOMB

THE MASTER AETHERIUS

"The release of atomic energy must have far-reaching meteorological effects. When an atom bomb is exploded, you have virtually a three-fold result:—

(1) heat, (2) radio-active waves, (3) etheric distortion, caused by the release of an energy which has hitherto been held in a state of potentiality.

"When an atom bomb is exploded, you have mass converted into energy manifesting itself as millions of degrees of temperature. It immediately vaporises all cloud formations in the vicinity, which are split up into their original gases, mainly oxygen and hydrogen. As well as this, thousands of tons of water from the sea are also taken up and vaporised. Because of that, water is changed back into gas, some if which is consumed by the heat of the explosion, but most of which is held in a state of suspension in a radio-active cloud which has now formed. The dangerous part, from a meteorological point of view, of this radio-active cloud, is the dense black smoke and dust that you can see and its subtler effects upon the ether. This ether is distorted by the strain of the suddenly released energy, which takes place within the natural filterisation belt surrounding Terra.

"The disturbed weather conditions just lately were due to hydrogen bomb explosions previously. The rain that fell then was slightly radio-active. If these explosions continue with their regularity then you will have enough radio-activity in the raindrops to be, in certain cases, extremely dangerous.

"Water is split up, from its combination, into atoms of hydrogen and atoms of oxygen. These are pushed from one part of the world to another by currents of wind, especially those freak winds which are a direct result of thermo-nuclear fission. These winds act as carriers for the thousands of tons of water now held in a state of suspension. Electro-magnetic storms combine these atoms, which fall down as radio-active rain.

"The whole atmosphere of the Earth is now and always has been radio-active. The whole atmospheric belt of your Earth is filled with minute atomic explosions, but these are under a control which has been pre-determined by natural mathematics, so as to afford you with only the rain that you need. It is obvious that any strain upon, or any distortion of the ether, caused by what is to you a little thing,—wrong thought—can cause droughts and famines or great floods. So obviously a tremendous play of etheric disturbances, such as that caused by the release of electro-magneto-motive power, which comes from the bombardment of unstable uranium 238 under high vacuum by slow neutrons, must have great effects upon the weather of your world.

"If atomic or hydrogen bombs were used in a future war, then all your rain would become radio-active and all your crops and cattle would die as a result of this, as well as all those people caught out in this radio-active rain. These would receive very severe burns. Your scientists have not yet found a cure for severe radio-active burns.

"It is vital that the indiscriminate release of this force is stopped. If your scientists could travel out into space and observe the world as a whole they would notice,

beyond any doubt that their little lunch-time parties at
Bikini were quite liable to cause the atmospheric belt of
Terra—severe gastric troubles.

"It is not my job to force a policy of nuclear embargo
—that must be brought about by those people upon
Terra *who are sensitive enough to have a conscience.*

"I would like to state here that the Planetary System
is a whole. Any indiscriminate material or etheric dis-
tortions indulged in, in any part of the System must, by
immutable Law, affect that WHOLE. As you continue
effecting nuclear fission through neutron bombardment,
you will approach a state where you have a saturation
of the ether through strains caused by radio-active
release.

"This can be simply illustrated in this way. If you
make an electric spark at point A, that electric spark
can be traced to point B. This is brought about because
the spark caused certain electric distortion which travelled in waves to point B and then, with an instrument
sensitive enough, it can be detected. Now, just for a
moment, suppose we have a great release of atomic
power within a certain area, then tremendous repercussions or etheric distortion must take place as a result
of this. Just as if you mix common salt with sea water,
you have very soon a saturated solution, so you have in
this illustration of mine, an etheric saturation caused by
strain or distortion of the ether, brought about by the
sudden release of radio activity. You see, if I hold this
hand here (placing Mental Channel's hand on the table)
I am not touching the atoms which constitute the table
top—it is not possible. I am touching the ether in
the table and these fingers, because there is more ether
in that hand and in that table top than there are particles of matter. If I haphazardly fire a projectile into
space, I have a million to one chance of hitting any

target, just as, when I hit the table like this I have a million to one chance of bringing together two particles of matter. The tension which holds together the ether, which in turn holds together the matter of this finger— tension brought about by the human mind— contacts the same tension which is brought about by the mind of the wood. You do not have a cohesion of particles in this simple case; you have an electrical and magnetic meeting of ether which is held in two different states. The sea of ether, in which exist the atoms of that finger, is distorted in a certain way. In another way, we have etheric distortion brought about by the release of various forces contained within the atom.

"Hydrogen bomb explosions cause a reaction similar to that on the Sun, namely the synthesisation of Helium from Hydrogen, but the Solar radiations have been specially prepared for by Nature. You have around Terra, a certain ionospheric belt which acts as a filterisation unit, to absorb and tone down cosmic rays. But a thermo-nuclear reaction *within* that ionospheric belt is something like transplanting a small Sun in the wrong place. The result is that you have deadly radiations just above the surface of the Planet where they can cause great havoc. But as well as this, you must have an un-natural multiplication of your existing filterisation units through ionisation which in turn will keep back vital Solar energy upon which all life on Terra is absolutely dependent.

"There is yet another important aspect of possibilities worthy of most urgent consideration. Some of you are no doubt conversant with the ancient study of Astrology and will realise the importance of emanations from the various Constellations. If these emanations are grossly affected, then you will have mutation on the psycho-mental and mento-physical levels.

"At the present time some of your scientists see a change taking place in the physical bodies of certain people. People are being born of neither one sex nor the other—animals are being born freaks. Plants are being brought into being in a freakish way. The change, up to the present, is slow and rather subtle; but if your complicated system of natural filters is disturbed too suddenly to a great extent, then you will have many hundreds of cases of physical mutation of man. You will have children born with two, three or four heads—I would rather not go into the ghastly details. This matter must certainly be taken into serious consideration.

"As a result of atomic release mutation will take place in the cellular structure of the human brain and this in turn will have its mental repercussions. Types of mentalities will suddenly be born, capable of attracting the kind of mind, which, at present, they are not ready to attract and they will use that mind very wrongly. Others will be born capable of attracting the lowest of all forms of mind—the negative minus type of mind—and they will be able to translate that mind and use it wrongly.

"This could have repercussions throughout the whole Planetary System! It is important that you should realise these things and as a result of this realisation, you should keep your minds under strict control. You should also teach your children to keep their minds under strict control, so that the factors which bring about mind mutation, however slight, cannot have such a disastrous effect. You are just as dependent upon the magnetic influences from Mars, Venus, Mercury, Saturn, Jupiter, Uranus, Neptune and Pluto as you are upon your grocer! I seriously ask all of you to consider this fact.

"Make no doubt at all, the situation as we see it on Terra is very serious—so serious in fact that we have spent many hundreds of hours in trying to put it right.

We have absorbed from your atmospheric belt a very great amount of what we will call 'static radio-activity' although it is not quite that. As a result you have missed several great meteorological calamities, which you would otherwise have suffered."

RADIO-ACTIVITY AND MUTATION*

Question:
"How does radio-activity cause idiocy and mutation?"
Author's note:
It must be indicated that the following reference to the glass is made after Aetherius caused His Mental Channel (George King) to pick up a tumbler which stood on the table before him.
The Master Aetherius:
"That glass will never be the same again—why?—because my friend here has touched it! What did he do when he touched it? Well he impressed *into* that glass the whole pattern of his characteristics. His likes, dislikes, the wildest flights of his imagination, even his tears, were all impressed upon the etheric spaces between the atoms of substance in that glass.

"Now there is a branch of science, known as psychometry, which has proved such things in many, many cases, to you Earth people. Well, now, if this is so—and the psychometrist will certainly go out of his way to prove that it is—through just a brief touch, how much more intimate, then, can the impression be, upon certain parts of the spermatozoa from man and woman. Such contact is, of course, extremely intimate. All characteristics are impressed. Each tiny molecule of that fluid is virtually a 'mirror' of the hopes, ambitions and failures of the particular person who excretes that fluid. THIS IS FACT! You have, then, the positive and negative genes uniting together to cause a magnetic field. Gradually around themselves are formed other masses of cellular structure—then in time you have a baby born. A baby having within it the characteristics of father and mother. Whether these remain as potential or are realised depends upon certain Karmic aspects.

"Now, radio-activity can and does alter the impression placed by the male and female upon the life cells. The subtler aspects of radio-activity do not travel through the atoms in the cellular structure but they operate by causing a specific strain upon the ether matter itself. Now, once this strain has been imposed by the centrifugal and centripetal co-axial magnetic forces, which are generated by the travail of radio-activity through the etheric matter in which the atoms themselves exist—the strain brings about change from the original pattern. This change can, in certain cases, when transferred and multiplied throughout the molecular mass which is to be the child, become a mutation. This mutation can manifest itself as idiocy.

"You have first of all an impression caused within the life fluid of the male, another impression caused within the life fluid of the female. These two combine to create a certain type of magnetic fluid. When these impressions are forcibly altered by abnormal strains, such as those travelling, as they do, through the finer etheric matter, they cause a strain or alteration of the existing pattern. The results are leukaemia, cellular mutation, cancer and idiocy."

*Reprinted from Cosmic Voice Issue No. 11 August/September 1957.

RADIO-ACTIVITY AND CANCER

The following extract is taken from Cosmic Voice,

Volume 1, page 31, an emergency appeal by Mars Sector 6, delivered on November 29th, 1955. This communication is included because it elucidates the terrible dangers of hydrogen bomb fall-outs.

MARS SECTOR 6

"This is Mars Sector 6 reporting. Subject:
The release of strontium through thermo-nuclear fission.

"We are concerned about the release of strontium 90 through thermo-nuclear fission. These strontium deposits will travel around your Earth and will settle in reservoirs and on arable land. Strontium has certain properties rather like calcium. It can be taken into plant and animal-life, so that, when this food is eaten by terrestrial people, the strontium will be absorbed directly into the blood-stream, nervous-system and the bone-structure— especially the latter. This will cause mutation of the bone-structure and cancer of the bone.

"Treat this seriously, for we are going out of our way to give you this information. I do not say that I represent the first source of this information. If you have been given it before, then I can only substantiate the danger of this. We know, because we are able to measure with very sensitive instruments the genetic effects of radio-active strontium released within the filterisation-units of Terra. Your scientists can measure one octave of radiation only —they know nothing of the SIX OTHER OCTAVES of this radiation.

"The people who hear of these things are entrusted with the mission of making them known to the populace. We should strongly advise you to go to any Spiritual lengths to bring this knowledge before the people in high places. Responsibility is then theirs. No Occult responsibility can be shirked without the incurrence of a large Karmic *debt*. Beware of this and—be helped by it."

Author's comment:

The day after this message was recorded it was an-
nounced by the B.B.C. that scientists in Paris had
discovered SEVEN TIMES the normal amount of radio-
activity in the atmosphere over France.

The Danger of Etheric Distortion

Later, at 9.10 p.m. on June 19th, 1957 the two great
Messengers from Mars—Mars Sector 6 and Mars Sector
8, gave to the world further startling revelations on the
dangers of etheric distortion caused by nuclear experimentation.

So important were these revelations considered to be,
that The Aetherius Society Headquarters in London,
England, sent out copies to every airport of note and all
civil airline companies on Earth.

If no action was taken by the authorities concerned in
the light of these warnings, then the blame cannot be laid
at the door of either The Society or The Cosmic Masters.
We all know that, since these warnings were issued,
numerous mysterious air crashes have shaken the world.

Never once have The Cosmic Masters been wrong in
Their timely advice and warning to terrestrial man—it
is man who, because of his scepticism, has let this Earth
down.

MARS SECTOR 6

"This is Mars Sector 6 reporting through General
Information Channel. Subject: *The danger of Etheric
distortion caused by nuclear experimentation.*

"The subtle aspects of radiation brought about as a
direct result of chain reaction are very much more dangerous, than the more apparent physical manifestations.

"There will be many cases of mysterious outbreaks of
fire throughout Terra. Unfortunately, many people who

travel through the skies of Terra in aircraft will be subject to disaster. Many fires in the past have been caused in aircraft, when they travel through particular concentrations of energy, brought about and brought together, as a result of magnetic pressure applied when the subtler emanations are thrown off by chain reactive principle.

"These energies converge over certain parts of the surface of Terra. This convergence of energy is very often brought about by the pressures exerted by mineral deposits—iron ore deposit, even if very deep beneath the surface, can cause a concentration of power of this type. As well as this, you have pressures exerted by the influence of other types of mineral deposit, sometimes in the vicinity. This causes the particular energy to be spun around in a vortex. This vortex of energy attracts to itself a type of subtle energy which can pass through mass. Because of its passage through mass, it alters slightly the etheric pattern impressed upon the ether matter in which exist the atoms which constitute the molecular make-up of the particular aircraft in question. The direct result of this magnetic interference and alteration of a predetermined pattern in the etheric fluid, is much heat. Therefore, it is possible for an aircraft caught properly in such a whirlpool of this force, to burst asunder, with, unfortunately, much loss of life.

"Many buildings upon the ground have suddenly burst into flames, in different countries of Terra. Some of them while torrential rain has been falling. These cases have been caused by the same type of power vortices which are, as I have stated, a direct result of chain reaction.

"If you go on, Terra, with large scale atomic and thermo-nuclear experimentation, the skies of your Earth will become extremely dangerous for your own traffic.

When you reach a certain saturation state, these power vortices will, by self imposed pressures, create a type of chain reaction and the power will be distributed throughout your skies. This, as you must admit, is not a pleasant thing. This, as you must admit, is even one more reason why atomic experimentation of all kinds, should be abolished.

Atomic experimentation and all types of radio-active experimentation, even for medical purposes, should immediately be abolished.

"This can quite easily be done with the exception only, for the present, of X-Ray apparatus. You have not yet replaced this with another type of apparatus to bring about the same result. I would strongly advise all Earth co-operators to impress upon their leaders the need to stop all types of radio-active experimentation, whether for alleged medical purposes or not, with the sole exception I have pointed out. Even though certain isotopes are used for diseases such as cancer, they themselves may result, apparently, in curing one cancer in one individual and doing very much harm to 200-300 individuals in the neighbourhood.

"You have already been given this type of information but some of the informants have suffered much. Because of this, you are, Terra, at the bottom of the Solar Class.

"This Transmission came from Mars Sector 6, through Mars Sector 8—General Information Channel. This Transmission came with the Sanction and Authority of Interplanetary Parliament. . . ."

MARS SECTOR 8

"This will I declare quite firmly. That all air disasters, which have come as a result of aircraft suddenly bursting into fire, are a direct result of radiation, in one way or another. We are familiar with the theory regarding bacteria being found in petrol tanks causing damage to fuel pumps. This bacteria has been given its essential motivating force by radiation, in one way or another. This is a definite statement coming from Mars Sector 8 —General Information.

"So to sum up, whether your aircraft suddenly burst into flames because of the failure of fuel pumps, caused by bacteria causing them damage or whether your aircraft suddenly burst into flames, caused by reasons hitherto unknown, I will say this definitely; that radiation in one way or another is the real cause, whether the source of that radiation be locked up in the radium vault of a cancer hospital or worse still, much worse still, whether it be the direct result of chain reaction. Many other mysterious fires have been caused by one or other of these things. Many, many more, will come in the near future, throughout Terra. We are sorry again, to have to make such announcement as this but we would like to remind our co-operators of the cause.

"Atomic radiation of all kinds is extremely dangerous to life of all kinds."

SATELLITE 216*

"We can measure all the octaves of manifestation, of this dangerous energy. Your very coarse geiger counters can measure one octave only. Our instruments already show a measurement of 13 trillion counts per 100th part of a second. These types of radiation are having a direct effect upon the subtle bodies of all people who pass on from their present existence to the other realms. It would be a fine lesson if all of you atomic scientists could really view your own subtle bodies now. If you could view the astral bodies of the many poor little children who died in Hiroshima and Nagasaki, this would teach you all a great lesson.

"Satellite 216, making this emergency appeal.

"This will I say to you gentlemen. The time will come when you will have to bear the negative counterpart of this particular Karmic manifestation. No matter how thick your concrete block-houses are, they will not protect you from this.

"I appeal to you to use your common sense, I appeal to you to have nothing whatever to do with any form of atomic experimentation, before it is too late, even to save yourselves. We are upon Terra, in a secret position, acting as Interplanetary Monitor for certain types of communication . . . I am from Jupiter . . . ."

*Reprinted from Cosmic Voice Issue No. 19 March/April 1959.

THE RUSSIAN ATOMIC ACCIDENT

The following Special Transmissions from Mars Sector 6 and the Master Aetherius were received in the usual way by George King, while he was in North Devonshire on April 18th, 1958—at 10.00 p.m.

It would appear that the accident which occurred in one of Russia's atomic establishments, had far-reaching repercussions. Not only were hundreds of workers killed but the release of radio-activity threatened the lives of 17,000,000—YES—SEVENTEEN MILLION—other people throughout the world.

Interplanetary Intelligences have repeatedly issued warnings against such a happening as this. Russia has received these warnings in special information releases, which were sent to Moscow and ALL other World Leaders—BEFORE this accident occurred.

Cosmic Voice had this to say to the Kremlin:*

"Sirs,—There is NO excuse for such a terrible occurrence. You have no ethical or moral right to carry on with any atomic programme which has the remotest chance of endangering the life of ONE person, NEVER MIND SEVENTEEN MILLION.

"You can thank God that the Space People have intervened to clear up the mess which you have caused.

"We appeal to your decency as human beings to take the ONLY course of action now left to you:

"STOP ALL ATOMIC EXPERIMENTATION IMMEDIATELY. GIVE THE FULL FACTS REGARDING THIS ACCIDENT TO THE REST OF THE WORLD.

"This accident could be one of the terrible shadows cast by a coming event which could be catastrophic, not only to Russia but to the world as a whole.

"In the cessation of atomic experimentation, as in every other field of human endeavour, co-operation is vitally necessary.

"It is Universal *co-operation* which can guarantee Peace—not Universal competition!

"It is the duty of ALL Earth Leaders to the peoples who depend upon their wisdom and sane judgment, to unite under the banner of world co-operation and stamp out this nuclear threat for ever. Unless this is done— the accident in Russia, terrible as it undoubtedly was, could be mild in comparison with those to come."

George King.

MARS SECTOR 6

"Owing to an atomic accident just recently in the U.S.S.R. a great amount of radio-activity in the shape of radio-active iodine, strontium 90, radio-active nitrogen and radio-active sodium, have been released into the atmosphere of Terra.

"This Transmission came from Mars Sector 6."

THE MASTER AETHERIUS

"All forms of reception from Interplanetary sources

will become a little more difficult during the next few weeks because of the foolish actions of Russia. *They have not yet declared to the world as a whole, exactly what happened in one of their atomic research establishments.* Neither have they declared how many people were killed there. Neither have they declared that they were really frightened by the tremendous release of radio-active materials from this particular establishment during the accident.

"Because this accident took place, we will most certainly have to use a tremendous amount of energy, which should be used in a very different way. We should not really have to expend this amount of energy clearing away dangerous radio-active clouds from the atmosphere of Terra. However, because of Divine Intervention, we are able to use enough energy in this direction to save about 17,000,000 lives, which otherwise would have been forced to vacate their physical bodies.

"Such were the far-reaching repercussions from this accident that we were given permission by the Lords of Karma to intervene! However, although we are at the moment intervening on behalf of Terra, in this direction, certain damage has already been done to large land and water masses!"

*Reprinted from Cosmic Voice Issue No. 16 June/July 1958.

"What the Scientists Say"*

"D. G. Arnott, Secretary of the Atomic Science Committee of the Association of Scientific Workers, referring to his laboratory at London Hospital, said this week:—

" 'There is an invisible film of radio-active dust on every piece of equipment in the room.

" 'Four years ago, I could go up on the roof and collect a can of non-radio-active rainwater. I can't today.'

" 'There has been a sharp rise in the intake of Strontium 90 in Britain since last year', he said. It now seemed doubtful if there was any 'safe' dose. ALREADY THOUSANDS OF PEOPLE WERE GOING TO DIE OF CANCER BECAUSE OF NUCLEAR BOMB TESTS.

" Every bomb dropped meant that an unknown number of children in the future would be still-born, idiots, or suffer from diseases and bodily malformations.

"This scientist also warned that medical experiments which might save human life were becoming impossible because of the increased 'background' of radio-activity from nuclear bomb tests.

"Professor D. G. Catcheside, of Birmingham University:—

" 'Even the smallest dose of radiation must have some genetic effect.

" 'Every mother-to-be is exposed to radiation at this moment, local radiation, heightened by bomb dust.

" 'It certainly could now be having an effect on premature births or still-births.'

"Professor J. Rotblat, Executive Vice-President of the Atomic Scientists Association, Professor of Physics in the University of London:—

" 'Already there is actual evidence of the presence of radio-activity in the bodies of people all over the world as the result of atom bomb tests held in the past three years.

" 'I have a graph showing the increase of radio-activity in my own body, although I have been nowhere near an atom bomb test.

" 'When the bomb explodes, radio-active particles are drawn into the higher atmosphere where they circle the globe many times before sinking to earth.

" 'The British hydrogen bomb to be tested soon at

Christmas Island will be exploded high in the air to avoid local effects. But the particles will come down eventually.'

"Dr. D. J. Strawbridge, M.A., B.Sc., D.Phil.:—

" 'Those who know the dangers and allow the folly to continue are guilty of a terrible crime against humanity.

" 'My fellow scientists say to me in private: 'It is madness, it ought to be stopped.'

"Sir Ernest Rock Carling, Consultant to the Home Office and Ministries of Supply and Health:—

" 'All potential parents ought to take the utmost care to avoid the accumulation of the smallest dose of radiation lest their children pay the penalty.

" 'The radiation sins of the father are visited on the children to many generations hence.'

"Professor Kathleen Lonsdale, Quaker Scientist; of University College, London:—

" 'I believe that radio-activity may be genetically affecting every mother-to-be now. Places where local radio-activity is significantly high would be the places to watch.'

"Colonel Geoffrey Taylor, former Professor of Medicine and Consultant Physician to the 14th Army:—

" 'Before we dash blindly into this—ill-informed, and with the public completely misled—we should demand more knowledge.

" 'Possibly 40 bombs can be exploded before the general world-wide radio-active danger point is reached, but many leading scientists believe that damage has already been done and it is precarious to explode further bombs.

" '*If the tests are not stopped before the danger point is reached it will be too late to prevent damage to three or four generations of mankind.*

" 'Assumptions about the action of radio-active strontium inside human bones may be disastrously wrong.

" 'Evidence available since the Medical Research Council's report was published shows the lethal effects of the contamination of man, animals and fish from radio-active material thought to be free of danger.

" 'Scientists agree that genetic damage is being done by previous H-Bomb tests and will be increased by the forthcoming British tests.'

"Professor Tadatoshi Doke, Japanese physicist, said this week that even with no more tests the safe dose of radio-active strontium for the world population as a whole will have been exceeded in five years.

"He has just completed an investigation into the dangers of radio-active dusts released by nuclear explosions.

"If tests continued at the present rate the dose rate in ten years would exceed the safety level for atomic workers.

"This is ten times what is considered safe for the population as a whole."

*The foregoing article originally appeared in Psychic News, April 13th, 1957.

CHAPTER IX

POSITIVE AND NEGATIVE

"Atom Particle Find Excites U.S. Physicists
"Anti-Proton Record*

"New York, Friday.

"A photographic record has been obtained of an atomic particle, apparently from outer space, which it is estimated moved at a speed and energy of ten thousand billion volts. The discovery has caused excitement among United States physicists.

"It was made by Dr. Marcel Schein, of the University of Chicago. He reported it to the American Physical Society yesterday.

"Dr. Robert Oppenheimer, the atomic scientist recently held to be a security risk by the Atomic Energy Commission, said that this was the physics problem to which he now intended to devote his time. 'It is trying to tell us something if we could read and understand it. Just what the particle is and what force it possesses nobody knows. When we understand what it is we will understand a lot more about the nature of physics.'

"Balloon Experiment.

"The particle was caught in an aluminium pack of special photographic plates carried in a high-altitude balloon over Texas last winter. It is reported to have torn through like a bullet through a pack of cards, but in doing so produced a scientifically thrilling picture, though to the ordinary eye it appears only as broken lines of dots.

"Physicists speculate that the particle is something

104

that nuclear scientists have been asking for years, an anti-proton. This is the opposite to a proton, the core of a hydrogen atom.

"In tearing through the film pack it is thought the anti-proton struck a proton and both were annihilated. For scientists the implication is that somewhere in the universe there exists a means of annihilating or converting into energy all the various kinds of matter known on earth.

"(Our Science correspondence writes—'The particle must have been travelling more than a million times faster than any speeded up by an atom-smashing machine and many hundred times faster than anything yet observed in nature. The discovery is bound to be of great importance')." *This article originally appeared in *The Daily Telegraph*—June 10th, 1954.

In view of the far reaching implications behind this discovery, the following questions were asked of Aetherius:

(*a*) "Were you responsible for putting that atomic particle in the hands of our physicists and (*b*) could you tell us more about it?"

THE MASTER AETHERIUS

"In answer to your first question, I would like to say that we did arrange to bring about this bombardment by an atomic particle, the like of which cannot be found upon this Earth of yours.

"We did this in order to give certain of your physicists a lead, so that this lead would help them to evolve, not only mathematical calculations, but also a philosophy superior to that which they hold at the present moment. We feel that certain of the physicists will know and recognise the fact that this particle cannot have been just floating about by chance, that in the beginning it must have been broken away from a molecular and atomic structure, because it is an anti-proton—a part of a particular kind of very fine matter not found in that way on Terra.

"In answer to your second question, first of all I would like to say that this is only one of many finds, some of which have not yet been published and more similar, apparently inexplicable, physical discoveries will take place in the future.

"You could do well to follow your newspapers very carefully, because certain information which is regarded as secret at present, will be brought more into view of the masses, through the medium of your press.

"I will tell you a little more about this particular thing. As you no doubt know, a proton is a positive positive.

"We, in this Planetary System, are all dependent upon Solar energy for our existence.

"The Sun is the absolute positive pole and generator of all positive energies in the Interplanetary System. Now then, an ordinary proton, such as that contained within hydrogen, which you regard as the simplest form of matter, is the positive core supplying a definite positive magnetic radiation to the rest of the structure.

"Therefore, if you obtain the exact opposite to that positive positive—a negative minus—you have something which is an anti-proton. Something which will fuse into the proton and thereby cancel out the amalgamated forces. During the process of cancellation in this case, however, there is an expression of unity which provides a release of certain energies.

"Now let us, in order to know more about this, get down to your ordinary thinking process. We have here an atom-splitting machine—the spine! Your Ancients said this and were indeed hundreds of years ahead of your modern physicists—very odd that your physicists should be so far behind! You have, within a certain part of your brain, the miniature of a tiny Sun which is your positive plus aspect. You have, within the base of your spine, something which may be described, for want of better terminology, as a tiny moon, which is the negative minus aspect. When the particles of these two energies meet, you have a fusion which is complete unity and the resultant expression or release of energy can be brought under very strict mental control. We all use this process of attraction, leading to implosion which designates the unity of forces in our daily lives. The result of this implosion becomes the opposite which is an explosion. Now action and reaction are opposite and equal; the reaction to the implosion, or very complete internal amalgamation of forces—is explosion. The result of this explosion on the mental level is a strain put upon the ether which in turn causes movement of a particle within the brain, which in turn is translated by impulse mechanism and finally you are able to translate this intricate process into sound or speech.

"You may be interested to learn that we adopt a somewhat similar process in the propulsion units of certain Flying Saucers—especially those which are used for extra-planetary journeys. Namely (a) attraction (b) implosion (c) reaction to implosion (d) explosion (e) control of energetic releases. The works of man are but copies of the Creator's Art. So we have copied a mental function which is inherent in everything, in the same way that you have made a copy of your nervous system and called it a telephone exchange.

"The discovery of the atomic particle by your scientists is the most important one made in all nuclear researches. I suggest that you meditate upon the fact that somewhere in the Planetary system there is a type of matter which, when fused into your matter, can completely cancel out the tension which holds together your molecular and atomic structure, thereby causing (1) great energetic release, (2) such a unity as to completely change the whole atomic structure of the Universe. When you consider this and meditate upon this, you should see what far-reaching Truth there is in this discovery of such a minute particle. It means that every positive proton in the whole of your Universe, has, in the Planetary System, its negative counterpart. Just as some of you have your male and female partners upon this existence, so has every positive proton its female negative counterpart. This is worth very due consideration, because acceptance of this one fact must broaden your outlook very greatly. That is why we allowed your balloon to receive this particular bombardment. You see, the Planetary system is much more of a unified Being or a Whole than would at first seem possible.

"Of course, we have to move carefully and in rather subtle ways, in order to impress those minds who are trying to control certain forces which are of rather a dangerous nature. So, a little atom here, traces of burning copper in the sky there, a few sightings here which cannot be denied and a few vague travelling lights there —this has been our policy. The time is not far away, however, when we shall adopt a more positive and more open approach, so that we can induce official circles to make correct statements to the public.

"Thank you! If you should wish to know any more about this particular aspect of our work, I would be only too pleased to enlighten you as much as my Advisors will allow. So I may wish you now Goodnight with this little thought—the surface of a pool may show a reflection, but that reflection is only surface deep. If you go beneath that surface, you find the reflection does not exist, but the picture which does exist is very different. Quite odd that some of your prominent people have not yet realised this. Of course, when they do, they will be included in the Planetary Government."

CHAPTER X

COSMIC LOGIC

THE MASTER AETHERIUS

"The time is coming when certain observers will notice a definite pattern in the sightings of Interplanetary Vessels. Up to the present time, only a few people in rather chosen positions have been able to work out the patterns, but this has been dictated rather by Cosmic necessities, which have cropped up, from time to time. We hope, most sincerely, that in the next year or so, the really interested observer will be able to denote our pattern of terrestrial reconnaissance.

"Now, I have said before, that we do not come to Terra with a new magic from the Planets, but we *will* offer our hands in friendship to those terrestrial beings who are ready to shake them. In certain cases, we have been able to tune in to groups of workers on Terra and have learned of certain necessities from these groups. We hope to be able to give you the knowledge so that these necessities can be brought into direct manifestation. All this takes a certain amount of time, of which you, in a way, are more conscious than we are. This is because, forgive me for saying this, we are able to see more of the pattern of evolutionary completion than you on Terra.

"You are not alone in your struggles—you have never been alone in your struggles for Spiritual supremacy. We have been aware, for centuries, of the tremendous battle now raging on Terra—a battle between basic materialism on the one hand, and Spirituality and enlightenment on the other hand.

"Now, when some of you regard the apparent surface chaos of your Planet, you are apt to be despondent. Cast this despondency to the winds, for it is a useless garment—it could never keep you warm because the winds of doubt could blow through its coarse weave and you would freeze.

"Discard your despondency!

"Have courage, hope and faith that your most honourable aspiration will be fulfilled by a greater magic than any other magic—the magic that is brought about by the power within you.

"Some time ago a single man from Earth stood upon a foreign planetoid and did face an evil monster. Blessings be upon his head, not only because he did Spiritual battle with this monster and released it from its evil, we could have done that without moving an inch from our Planet, but because he had faith in the power within himself. (See Chapter IV).

"This is the crux of my message: know yourselves and help yourselves—you cannot help yourselves without knowing yourselves, it is absurd. The more you know yourselves and help yourselves, the more you will be helped from all sources. Go out of your way to help and teach others and the more you do so, the more you will be helped to do this, for it is an honourable calling.

"You will find that in the coming years, the Flying Saucer believers will be split into two camps. One lot will look upon them from the super-mathematical aspect and the other camp will look beyond the products of mathematics—to the Light. It is to this latter camp that I have to speak, in order to teach and help.

"The other camp will be looked after by other agents, trained specially to look after the more academically minded terrestrial beings. So we will spread the teaching throughout this dark island which we call Terra—an

island only because you have deliberately cut yourselves
off and tried to shut away the Light of knowledge, which
cometh through the ethers.

"I hope you will stay this dissection and open yourselves to those Cosmic rays which are being emanated by
the Planetary Beings, so that you may become warm in
the depth of winter, Light in the darkness, Holy in the
midst of sin, pure and clean in the midst of impurity and
dirt.

"You can do it now, if you will—it is not impossible
for any of you. If I knew one here who would find it
impossible, I would not talk so. If each one of you expended
the correct effort, you could become filled with Cosmic
Light and knowledge, for it would be the right knowledge
which has been passed through the heart and moulded
into wisdom. That cold knowledge, which has limitations,
is useless because, sooner or later, it must be transmuted
into something higher. So why not start in the right place
now, gain the knowledge, pass it through the feelings and
bring it into being on the Planet for yourselves ?

"If you try to do this, you will not be working by yourselves—many others will see to that. It is the Occult Law
that the teacher himself must not trespass upon the
private sanctuary of what may be termed a person's individual way of thinking. But if the thinker transmutes his
way of thinking to the highest realm of which he is
capable, then can the right teacher shed Light into his
mind and body and raise him up.

"This is so—it has happened before on Terra—your
great Masters have done this. Your Great Masters chose
to be born in material poverty. I am informed that there
is one shining exception to this—Buddha—who serves
only to prove the rule—and even then, He had to cast
aside His materialistic accumulation *before* He could
receive the Light.

"I must point out that it is easy to make excuses and say, 'If I had been born so-and-so, I could have done better', but this is not so, it is the foolish talk of a child. Each and everyone of you can, in the quiet of your own room—which is your mind—draw inspiration which comes from within. The more people who do this, the more will follow those people, because they will see within you the Light—they may not know that they see it, but they will see it. They will not know why, but like moths that flit around the light of your lantern, they will follow. Why should the Law suddenly change now? It has been the vogue for 3,000 million years upon Terra and it will be 3,000 million years more before the Planet is absorbed back again into the Sun.

"The evolution of mankind is now being speeded up, in order to reach a certain point within a certain time limit. Co-operate with the speeding up, help it, become the beings who speed this up and I promise you a million helpers. If you do, you will never regret any time you have spent in this wonderful way. There is so much for all of you to do, but so little time in which you can do it. Then strike the gong of the present, so that the echoes may be magnified by the future. These are the teachings which we, from the Interplanetary Governmental Systems wish you to take, absorb, believe and act upon. Then we can make our next move, which will be free movement among you and direct help given in your schools, universities, hospitals and governments. If you go out of your way to reach up to us, we can and we will come out of our way down to you, but you must move! We cannot come unless you do this—that is the Law. We do not break the Law.

"He who knows the Law of God and breaks it is the biggest fool ever born. There is only one Law—the Law of God. Whatever is truly good, must be truly and honourably within the confines of the Law, as laid down by Beings, greater even than the Solar Logos. What will you do—listen to the mathematicians, or to such Beings as these? Make your choice! Ponder well, accept, if you are ready. Reject—and you put yourselves back. Why do this? Go forward and mould the future. To-day is the to-morrow you made for yourself yesterday.

"We are on the verge of a new terrestrial age during which the Ancient teachings will be presented in a more modern way. Your theatres and your broadcasting system will be used by those few who have the Light within them. (Note 1). See how powerful they can be! See what strength they wield throughout the Cosmic System. Never before, in the history of this Planet were people called upon, as they are being called upon to-day! Every Initiate is being called upon to do his best. Every disciple, every follower is being called upon to do his part too. So do it and know that you cannot fail.

"If you fail then God would fail.

"If you say this is possible, then I must smile in unbelief. Your books say that the Light of God Never Fails —it never has done and it never will!

"If you want one impossible thing, this is it—all else is possible.

"The very fact that you were interested enough to come to-night proves the stirring of conscience within you. Heed it and let it be your guide, your teacher, your illuminator and you cannot go wrong. You can lead the world from the dark chaos that your atomic scientists and your materialists have put it into, up to the shining Light of Bliss, which is so wonderful as to be beyond all description. Surely you would not sit with your foot in a naked flame—you would move yourself away if you could. Why sit shivering in the cold darkness of ignorance which you yourselves have fabricated for yourselves, when you have only to raise your mind to that thing, that indescribably beautiful thing, that real thing, that true thing, that flame, that inspiration, that wisdom, that love, that perfection which is within your very souls at this very moment?

"I must go now. I have other duties to perform this evening, so I leave you, and ask you to ponder upon my words—the more you ponder, the more you will get from them, I promise you that. These are simple words, but the greatest truths are the simplest ones. God is the Eternal Simple. Complications mean deviation from Simplicity. Simplicity is Oneness. Deviation from Oneness is acceptance of duality. Duality is changeable—like time. That which is changeable is not Reality, therefore belief in Oneness is the essence of the Acceptance of Reality. Now, as Reality is God and God is eternal, therefore, God is the only Eternal Simple in the whole Macrocosmic System.

"This, my friends, is Cosmic Logic."

NOTES:

Note 1

Since this statement was made, the Author has appeared 7 times on Television in Britain. He also demonstrated an actual Transmission from The Master Aetherius, Who spoke to the British public over B.B.C. Television during the programme—"Lifeline", on Thursday, May 21st, 1959. (See Cosmic Voice Issue No 20—page 28.)

The Author appeared 46 times over radio and Television in the U.S.A. and Canada. He also gave an actual Transmission where again, The Master Aetherius spoke to California on the Tom Duggan Show, station KCOP, Hollywood, July 19th, 1960. He gave a $5\frac{1}{2}$ hour interview over station WOR, New York, February 19th, 1960.

During his intensive five week Australian trip, The Reverend George King made no less than 17 radio and Television appearances in Sydney and Melbourne alone.

CHAPTER XI

RELIGIOUS RE-ORIENTATION

THE MASTER AETHERIUS

"In our humble estimation, it is essential that the teaching of Re-incarnation should be accepted and indeed put over throughout your major religions on Terra in this coming age.

"This teaching will provide the answer to many problems, which up to now have not been fully answered by your religious leaders. They lose a major following because of their inability to answer quite simple questions, such as 'why is so-and-so mentally deficient while his brother is a clever child.' They can answer this properly, only, by propounding the Truth of the Law which governs life, Truths which have been brought into being regarding those things which have necessitated Karma.

"My Advisors, who have travelled your Earth quite a bit, tell me that many religious leaders in the Western regions of Terra actually know of the existence of the Law of Re-incarnation. Those people who know of these things and yet are not prepared to teach them, are guilty of a foul crime—a subtle one admittedly, but nevertheless a major crime. You have been told through countless ages that the greatest gift you can give to another man is to teach him how to reach up to that thing you call God. So, therefore, these people are lacking in their duty to their followers and to the world as a whole.

"The time will have to come when the Western religious leaders and teachers will have to take from Oriental teachers certain things which are acceptable to

116

them and put them into practice. Theory is no good without practice; what good is it? It is useless. So our message to your religious leaders throughout the Western world is to be prepared to introduce into your teachings, Truths about Re-incarnation, so that you can give your followers a better, truer and more understandable picture of the Law which is God.

"If you leaders try to wrap this up, to hide it beneath a bushel, then you must be prepared to give up your positions to those people who are braver. The coming age demands bravery in all respects. I tell you this: no man or woman can realise One-ness without bravery. So all religious leaders must be brave enough to break away from the dogma which is only a small part of the Truth and be prepared to use the best which comes out of the East so that it can be practised in the West. The theory of the East and practice of the West is the perfect union; that is what we are trying to bring about in the New Age. We are trying to get the major factors in the West to put into practise the Ancient wisdom which dawns with the rising Sun.

"My friends, your presence here denotes that you have accepted a grave responsibility, the responsibility of breaking up the dogmatic nonsense which only adds to ignorance and confusion throughout Terra. You can help in this work to the best of your ability and so try to introduce the Truth.

"Now, it would appear that your religious leaders will fight to hang on to the dogmatic nonsense, pardon this term but I cannot think of a better one, which they have held on to for hundreds of years. I will now quote my Mental Channel who says, quite rightly, 'When a man knows the Truth and knows that the Truth will give him power and will not pass on that Truth to another—not because the other is not ready, but because he does not

wish the other to have the same power that he has—
such a one is no better than the aboriginal witch doctor.'

"The time has come when certain cherished founda-
tions must be torn up by the roots and cast onto the fire
of discriminating Truth to be transmuted. The religious
leaders of Terra have this responsibility in the coming
age. Your Bible has to be re-written. It has to contain
more of the Truth in a more understandable way than
it does at present.

"It is the age of science. The greatest science upon this
or any other Earth is the study of God. The greatest
science upon this or any other Earth is religion. What
greater study can there be? Knowledge of the real
governing unchanging Laws brings man freedom from
ignorance, freedom from want, freedom from disease,
freedom from pain, freedom from the horrors of war,
freedom from the baser aspects of his own mind and freedom from the prison created by materialistic accumulation—the most subtle prison of all. This is the only thing
that will bring these freedoms. There is no other way to
get them.

"If the Law of Re-incarnation was studied first and
taught properly afterwards, then you would see war
gradually die out on this Planet. A man would not go to
war if he thought he may be killing someone who has
been his own brother, his own blood relation, in a past
life. The love of God, that some of you talk about so
freely, can be made to *live*, can be made a vital existing
thing upon Terra by the correct teaching of the basic
Laws.

"I would say here and now that the religious teachers
who are in high positions are doing themselves not only
great injustice, but great personal harm. No, I would go
further than that; I would say they are doing the world
a great harm by withholding this most essential teaching

at this time. So much Light is being poured upon this Earth that this Light will penetrate into the darkest corners of the mysterious archives and will cause these to be revealed to man. If the religious leaders were to reveal these now, in the correct way, they would keep their followings, they could fill their churches with people who wanted to go and pray for their brothers.

"If they do not reveal these things now, then these things will be revealed by other Leaders who will empty the churches throughout the world. They will have meetings upon the tops of hills and in barns.

"We feel rather strongly about this, because religion is the one method which has not been tried by Terra, yet it is the only method that can really succeed. By religion I do not mean dogma, I mean the real teachings of the Law. Not those foolish things made by man but the Laws laid down by the Great Architect of the Galactic System; Laws which are immutable and unchangeable and whether you agree with them or not, you have to accept them and abide by them. Any deviation from the path laid down by these Laws has its repercussions upon those people who deviate. There is no doubt at all about this.

"You see, we believe, after a certain study of Terra, that if your religious leaders took a brave step forward into the light of the New Age, they could bring about a great rise in consciousness which could put your people above such useless things as war, could rule out famine and alter the educational system of your world, could transmute your present-day economic system up to a place of brotherly subsistence.

"It is essential that all of you who are willing to follow, must try in your little way to get this type of message over to your religious leaders. If it does not do any good, then at least you have tried; you can detach yourselves from the result, but do not belittle your own ability in this respect. If you go forward armed with the sword of Real Truth—not the Truth you like to pick from Truth, but the whole Truth whether you like it or not—armed with this weapon whole worlds will tremble before you, even though you may not be aware of the fact. If it comes to a battle between good and bad, good will always win; it always has and it always will. Although bad is appearing to win, it is only because there is an allowance in the Law made for this appearance. Meditate on these words— *for this appearance.*

"The time has now come when terrestrial man must recognise the fact that he is beginning the journey back out of the coarse matter of materialism to the Love which is God. How better can this be accomplished than by right teachings from religious leaders, throughout the world.

"The new Avatar, who has not yet come to Earth but will shortly do so, will teach these things. You can imagine the battle He will have when the time comes. Some of your followers, like the Mental Channel who is tuning into my emanations, have been chosen to go forward to form an outpost, so that the way may be prepared. If you push your wedge of Light into the darkness, it will prepare the way for that which is to come, rather like a snowplough going first and a big food lorry following along afterwards. You see, the food would never reach the people if the snowplough had not prepared the way; so it is with Spiritual things.

"In conclusion, therefore, I must say that we have this message for the religious leaders of Terra in the coming age.

"You must put forward correctly, truthfully, without alteration or adulteration, the teachings of Re-incarnation. If you fail, then your own communities will displace you. You will be displaced by what you may term unorthodox teachers who will arise. These unorthodox teachers will not need great churches or cathedrals for they will meet under the blue dome of Heaven and raise their voices to the trees. And I say unto you, that all the world will hear them. They will make far more commotion than do your church bells make on a Sunday morning!

"The time has come when we feel that it is essential that these things should be brought to the notice of you religious leaders. Each one of you has responsibility for the position of the world at the present time and none of you can divorce yourselves from this responsibility. The responsibility of the ordinary man, grave as it is, is not as grave as the responsibility of you religious leaders. Act upon this, realise it, execute your responsibilities properly, or evolution will displace you!"

CHAPTER XII

QUESTIONS AND ANSWERS

The Sun and Atlantis

Question: "Was the Sun nearer to the Earth in the time of Atlantis, than It is now?"

Aetherius: "The Sun was 18,456,962 miles further from the Earth than It is now."

Question: "Why is this?"

Aetherius: "The Sun is cooling and in the process of cooling, It must get hotter. This will happen, because It will first start to swell, then start to contract. This is because of particle cohesions within the present atomic and molecular structure of the Sun Itself. The process is timed to finish in the distant future and because of this, a slight variation in the relation and position of Terra and the Sun has occurred over these last centuries."

Question: "Did the Atlanteans use the Sun for their colour healing?"

Aetherius: "Yes, they did use Solar energy for this purpose. They recognised the potential of Solar energy and brought this potential into activation by a process of tuning into and storing Solar energy but it will be very difficult for you to understand exactly how they did it."

Question: "I understand it was stored in towers and a certain glass used, which cannot be used today. The glass was cut into particular shapes, which gathered the rays and the power from the Sun."

Aetherius: "You are correct, though it was not glass but quartz, ground and shaped in a certain way. These specially prepared quartz shapes put a tension upon the ether as the Sunlight passed through them and that tension remained in a particular portion of the ether, as it were. The ether was 'scrambled' and when they wanted to use this energy, they unscrambled the ether. I understand that you can scramble wireless messages, so that others cannot understand them and the receiver can record them and unscramble them again when he wishes. This bears a slight resemblance to the action of the quartz colour batteries."

Question: "Were plates made of this material?"

Aetherius: "Plates, as you call them, were thought up by a scientist priest—these Atlantean priests were the scientists. During this process of molecular cohesion, brought about by mental stresses, a certain emanation from the mind of the priest entered into these multi-shaped materialised containers, which could store the etheric stresses referred to earlier—which were scrambled Solar energies—for future use in the winter time."

Question: "What bearing has the position of the Sun upon us at the present and what is its exact distance from the Earth now?"

Aetherius: "The Terra-Solar distance has a certain deep abstract bearing upon human existence at the present, the significance of which you will discover when you have evolved and studied the Occult sciences. However, one who is travelling through time, with a physical body, the atoms of which would need to be held in a state of suspension during travel, would have to be careful of his calculations, especially when he reached his predetermined goal. If he had not allowed for the exact change in the Solar position, relative to the time alteration, when he amalgamated and cohesed the molecular structure back into its original shape, the atomic structure could quite well be changed by Solar radiations.

"I will not divulge the exact distance between the

Sun and Terra. If your scientific instruments were as delicate as ours, this figure could quite well mean the difference between success and failure. However, 93,500,000 miles is good enough for the effective limits in which your mechanisms are capable of travail. You know, it is upon the higher levels of mento-physical projection, that lie the greatest dangers. I have met three men upon Terra, who asked this same question. Only one was ready for this secret answer—which enabled him to visit the Sun."

SPACE-CRAFT AROUND EARTH

Aetherius: "I seem to be the centre of much activity, which demands certain thanks."

(He was referring to the placing of the microphone in position, to record His answers.)

"I think my time may be short but I am willing to try, to the best of my ability, to answer relevant questions."

Question: "I notice that you have said in the past, that we are as dependent upon emanations from other Planets, as we are upon our grocer. What type of emanations do other Planets receive from Earth?"

Aetherius: "The Planetary System as a whole, is rather like one family. Now, in a family, because the children have issued from a common womb—the mother's—they have an electro-magnetic link with this womb and also with each other. The Planets have issued from the Sun and therefore have a common electro-magnetic link with the Sun and thus with each other. Now, the Earth, to put it simply, is a very basic Planet, so that the colour emanating from the Earth, is of a very basic nature. Plant life on Mars, receives those colours from Terra, which promote their growth."

Question: "Are radio waves emitted from Venus and Mars and also from Space Ships?"

Aetherius: "I believe that, in exceptional conditions certain ultra-short-wave radio transmissions have been endeavoured and in one particular place upon your globe, regular ultra-short-wave communications are carried on between X-90 and a group of Occult scientists. In the near future XB-70, which is the number of our second Satellite in space above the Earth, will contact certain radio receiving stations. We hope to use high speed Morse code through a scrambler. The receiving station is already standing by.

"We have two Satellites in Space between Luna and Terra. From these Satellites observers note many changes taking place on Terra. These Satellites are artificial moons which we have built, in order to have some observatories which can keep your Earth under close surveillance. Now, it is from one of these Space Stations that International Morse signals have already been received by Earth and we are going to transmit from the other. I am afraid that I cannot tell you the Earth receiving stations yet for very obvious reasons."

Question: "Should we be able to see these Satellites from the Earth?"

Aetherius: "They can and have been detected by radarscope. The American, Australian, New Zealand, Indian, Russian and British Governments all know of the Satellites' existence. They cannot always be seen with the naked eye because sometimes we have bent light rays round them to keep them invisible. Under certain ecliptic angles, however, they have been denoted by radio-telescopes."

Question: "How were they made—by vibration?"

Aetherius: "All is vibration. We made these on Venus, de-materialised them and brought them to a predetermined spot which would suit us and then re-materialised them again."

Question: "When did this take place?"

Aetherius: "About four-and-a-half Earth years ago, our first Earth Satellite was in position but we have, in the past, at various times, had Space observatories in similar positions."

Question: "How do you break out of lines of force when your Satellites are encircling the Earth and how do you get them into place?"

Aetherius: "We have overcome the Law of Gravity, therefore we have no undue stress or strain put upon our bodies, even when we travel at 4 million times the speed of light, which is the speed of thought in free space."

Question: "Are the Satellites of earthly substance?"

Aetherius: "They are made of organic metal, which would replace itself if a piece was broken off. It answers very quickly to thought—that is why we use it. It is a creation of mind. We have advanced a step further than your scientists—we have created a substance out of the boundless supply of energy which will withstand Cosmic bombardments without deterioration, hence the use of organic metals."

Question: "The person from Venus, who was seen by Adamski, refused to be photographed. Can you tell us why?"

Aetherius: "We have an intelligence system which operates amongst you and photographs are always a means of identification. There are other reasons which I cannot disclose—just now."

Question: "Are you using the Moon as a base?"

Aetherius: "We have a base upon Luna and from there, rays are projected which help us greatly in our work."

Question: "Are you using the dark or the light side of the moon?"

Aetherius: "We are using both sides of Luna but we use the side facing Terra, for observation. The bridge on the Moon has been fabricated by us and its action is a magnetic one. It draws together certain prevalent magnetic fields and when we are there, we can use this power, which is held in a state of suspension. Your Stonehenge had a similar use centuries ago."

Question: "Could we do these things on Earth now."

Aetherius: "Yes."

Question: "We would like to—but what is lacking in us?"

Aetherius: "I think we may say *Absolute* Belief in God."

DEGREES OF MIND

Question: "I have heard of a Planetary communicator called 'Oriel'. Do you know anything about this?"

Aetherius: "The name 'Oriel' is probably some name given to a Martian communicator by an Earth man. The name itself is not from our language but that does not invalidate the information. You see, telepathy is rather on a par with ordinary radio communication and just as you have interference in your radio reception, so also you have interference in your telepathic translation. As I have said before, I want you to beware of any communicators who call themselves 'chief' this, that or the other. The communicator who is anything at all is generally known by a simple name, or a name which you yourself have given him."

Question: "In the possible event of a third World war or World cataclysm, would certain individuals be removed, beforehand, from Terra? If so, would they be removed by Space-ship, in their physical bodies, or be dematerialised and re-materialised elsewhere?"

Aetherius: "Yes, we would pick up *certain factors* from Terra and transport them to other Planets. We would not pick up *all your great Masters* because if we did, the

World would immediately crumble into dust. So marked is the difference between the thoughts of the Great Masters and those of the ordinary man, that were all the Masters taken away from Terra the ordinary people would soon have a universal calamity, which they could not survive."

Question: "If some of the human beings from Terra should go to Venus or Mars, would a city have to be built for them—self-contained with a special atmosphere?"

Aetherius: "Yes, for a time. Afterwards, it would be possible to overcome the trouble by a process of transference of life from one body to another. I have just been told that certain of your Masters in Thibet can do that; they make a fluidic body and then withdraw the vital life-force from the physical body and inhabit the fluidic body. These are called Shades. The subtler bodies would not be effected by such a small change in environmental conditions.

"I do not want you to think I may be pouring cold water on your ideas—only down the throat of the medium. (The Great Teacher caused George King to take a sip of water.) Four hundred and twenty-five colours are coming from this liquid and if you were advanced enough to be *allowed to live on other Planets*, you would be able to see the colours quite clearly. Our psychic centres work perfectly and our eyes do not work on a refracting principle. We can tune into things directly and draw vital information from them."

Question: "What is the average span of life on Venus?"

Aetherius: "It depends on your state of consciousness; we have certain Masters who live from five thousand to seven thousand years and can live longer in the same body, if they wish. On Saturn they can live twenty-five thousand to fifty thousand years, in the same physical body, if they wish."

Question: "It is true that the Planet Venus is in its seventh round or seventh phase of existence, the final one before the great Pralaya?"

Aetherius: "Yes it is so. It has been absorbed six times and there will be a seventh absorption. After that it will be brought out again upon a higher plane of existence."

Question: "Would it be possible for us to meet a Flying Saucer, by appointment, very soon?"

Aetherius: "That is a good question. Certain of you are already chosen to meet us personally."

Question: "Can you give us a little about the comparative chemistry of the physical bodies used on Venus? Is there any comparison with our chemistry of carbon compounds, for instance?"

Aetherius: "It is rather complicated because a lot of us exist in subtle states and when we come to this Planet, or to Mars, or any other World, we build for ourselves a body to live on that Planet. If the people of that particular Planet have twenty-seven legs, as some people have in the Milky Way, then we can build a body with these twenty-seven legs. If carbon is the basic cellular property, we can use this by drawing it out of the atmosphere and blending it in such a way as to form a cellular structure, in harmony with environmental conditions prevalent upon the particular Planet we are visiting. On the other hand, we can use a silicon base; certain plants have a silicon base. There are few people on Venus who use bodies of a coarser matter and these only when necessary—yet we are physical beings.

"It is not possible for me to give English names, for the constituents of the molecules of the subtle bodies, because you have no words to describe them. So tenuous are these bodies, that it would be like giving a name to the molecules of your Soul, as it were. It would be impossible to do that, unless you had a language like certain of the Planets with 25,000 symbols in the alphabet. That language is never written."

Questions: "What foreign tongue have you used on certain occasions, is that Venusian?"

Aetherius: "It is one of the basic tongues, (He speaks in strange language). You are welcome to that, for what it is worth; it is only variation of sound. I am making these sounds through an Earth larynx but through our Venusian larynx it would sound very different."

Question: "In your printed writing, do you have a large alphabet, with 400 characters or a smaller one?"

Aetherius: "We have a fairly large alphabet. We must have this in order to impart certain more basic information, but the highest Teachings and the highest philosophical concepts are not written, they are *thought* about. We do not write as much as you do, because we believe that the right education is the education that man can give to himself. When certain psychic centres are opened, this causes the brain to pick up higher vibrations—aspects of mind and translate them, so that they are understandable. This is the right type of education and in this way, we do not need the tons of written matter that you do on Terra."

Question: "We do not need half of it!"

Aetherius: "I understand that many people make a lot of money out of it."

Question: "You spoke just now of the brain picking up vibrations on a higher level. The ordinary man has several organs radiating frequencies of a specific type from each organ. The heart may have a particular frequency and in good health the frequency is changed. How?"

Aetherius: "When I speak of the brain, I mean the whole brain, not just the molecular structure in the head, that is the culmination of it, but the spinal column is also a brain, as well as a power house.

"Now, mind has different aspects and different frequencies and the lower mind is picked up by lower centres, which have a particular type of power of attraction and this attracts its like. The higher aspects are picked up by the higher psychic centres, through which mind enters. All these things vibrate within a particular framework. When I talk of the psychic centres, I do not mean that a psychic centre is within the heart; I mean that the heart is the physical counterpart of the subtle centre, which is within the subtle bodies."

Question: "Then does it mean that there is a physical heart vibrating at its own frequency and its etheric or higher vehicle has its chakra vibrating on a different frequency?"

Aetherius: "There is a correspondence between these frequencies and there is a very close liaison—you might almost call it an *innate understanding* between these frequencies. Both are within a certain framework and when a person becomes more advanced so this changes; it changes with his evolution. It changes through his experiences and he is then able to attract and understand the higher aspects of mind. All Planetary mind is one and it is quite possible for you to sit down and meditate and know what is happening on some Planets. If your different brains are sensitive enough, you can do this. They are sensitised by evolution. What is evolution? Evolution is experience, so brains are sensitised by experiences of different types and by the repetition of these experiences. They are sensitised by the experience gained by living through these experiences. These are the things that give you the essential sensitivity necessary in order to pick up and understand the ˌhigher aspects of mind.

"At the present time, you are all being bombarded by the very high, very fast magnetic impulses of *All mind* but you can only understand those travelling slowly; the im-

pulses travelling at a faster rate are too subtle to be understood by you. So it is up to you to develop sensitivity and
have experiences as quickly as possible. Your Spiritual
exercises will help you. You are told that you will have
certain experiences of a Spiritual Nature and you do so.
You would normally need to live thousands of years, in
order to gain this evolutionary advancement. It is essential and necessary that you practise diligently and have
these experiences—some of which are pleasant, some are
unpleasant! Write them down, try to remember them
and live through them again and again, until you fully
understand them. Then you will pass on above them.
You are all the time sensitising yourselves to the highest
aspects of Planetary mind. Do you understand? Just as
the centre here (pointing to throat of Mental Channel)
is working a little above the normal speed and is rather
compressed, so is such experience compressed.

"Thank you for your kind attention and your curiosity.
You say it killed the cat—but it also educated the King."
Question: "Telepathy has died out to a certain extent, due
to advanced civilisation, yet You, who are more advanced
than we, use telepathy. Why is this?"
Aetherius: "If the lunch-time parties at Bikini are a
measure of civilisation then we are savages! Thank Holy
God! Civilisation as you know it is, in some respects, another name for crimes committed with a velvet glove.
Hypocrisy is called diplomacy. Foolish repression in
children, is called education, changeable materialism is
called reality—how strange, how perfectly odd!

"I have tuned my senses to the feelings of the Mental
Channel and I find that he is suffering from many com-
plaints which go with modern civilisation.

"You are quite right. We do use telepathy. When this
world settles down and puts things in their rightful places,
then you will have schools giving instruction on the en-

hancing of the existent but latent telepathic abilities. *You are not ready, in spite of and because of, your civilisation, for such an educational renaissance.*"

Question: "Do you have agriculture on Venus?"

Aetherius: "That question could quite well be lectured upon. If you mean in the way that you have it on Terra, the answer is 'No'. We do have a more highly evolved form of agriculture. You see, we know that certain plants have to gain experience, therefore, we go out of our way to rear these plants in perfect environmental conditions so that they can gain the necessary experience. That is why we go to great lengths if some of our plants have diseases, because we wish to help these living creatures over their Karmic periods and we are able to enhance their experience."

Question: "Do you grow these plants to eat?"

Aetherius: "It is necessary only for the lowest forms of life on Venus to consume material food. The majority of the inhabitants, live on Solar energy and we have also tapped the Mighty and Holy Source of the Goddess of Venus. We have tapped the outpourings of the Supreme Logos of the Planet, which gives us Spiritual food. Spiritual food, if you are correctly attuned, can sustain the body."

Question: "That is an accomplishment which certain people on Earth acquired—Mr. Gandhi, for instance."

Aetherius: "It would appear that you are quite correct in your observations. Yes, I understand that certain advanced souls upon Terra can and do live as we can."

Question: "The small proportion of Venusians who consume food, what is their function?"

Aetherius: "You too have an animal kingdom like us. Only the animals eat food on Venus but you see, to us they are all the same family.

"There is really little distinction between all of you and a fish or a rattlesnake and when you become correctly educated to this feeling of unity, you will be able to do the things that we can do. Until this complete acceptance of terrestrial unity is brought about, great limitations will be yours. Your own Universe will not wholly co-operate with you.

"Unlock the door of your inner knowledge by exploding the forces of intuition on the Super-conscious level and there you have the highest form of meditation."

COSMIC PHYSICS

Question: "Can you describe the various types of Flying Saucers used?"

Aetherius: "There are several types of vessels used by us from Venus. First, the Mother Ship, which conveys the small patrol vessels to within a certain radius of the Earth. This position varies according to the prevailing magnetic field, which is quite often changed by the position of Luna and also by certain conditions prevailing upon the Sun. You may say that it is our usual procedure to bring the Mother Ships to within 500 to 1,000 miles of the Earth but occasionally it is essential to bring them nearer than that.

"The Mother Ships vary in size: some are over 500 miles long and these large ones can travel outside of the Planetary System to various sections of the Milky Way and also to other parts of the Cosmos. Mother Ships which are mainly used for Interplanetary travel are about 1,000 yards upwards. Mother Ships of the smaller variety, carry seven small patrol vessels. Large Mother Ships, can carry up to 7,000: these ships are rather like cities and can remain away from base for years if necessary.

"From the Mother Ships, the smaller patrol vessels may go out. There are four major types of patrol vessels: some are remote-controlled, others are manned, some carry a crew of five, some a crew of four and some only two. The usual type of 35½ foot vessel carries a crew of two, and the larger Flying Saucers carry a crew of five.

"We have also vessels which carry the Masters; these are often invisible and they can come within the scope of your radar and yet be undetected. It is sometimes necessary for the Masters to travel thus. They carry with them certain pupils on the verge of Ascension. The Masters also use this type of vessel when they are Spiritualising your Earth. They come in these vessels to a certain part of your world and the Spiritual radiations that emanate from Them bring about a rise of consciousness. They also affect the rate of vibration of the atomic structure of not only that part of the world on which they are operating, but also the vibratory rate of ALL matter which is contained in that part of the world. So, in order to do this, they use a special vessel."

Question: "Can you tell us about speeds and time involved in Space travel?"

Aetherius: "It depends upon the operators. If they are all Masters, then it will take 2·3 seconds from Venus to Earth, so we travel fairly quickly. If the operators are younger ones, then the speeds may be lowered to the speed of light, or a little over. However, even the younger ones can exceed the velocity of light and that is, of course, in a vessel that we regard as being physical."

Question: "Is it by the power of thought that the Saucers obtain their power of propulsion?"

Aetherius: "In a way. For some of the vessels used we have a mechanism. Now as you no doubt know, if you make a noise, that noise gives off sound and colour. The colour, the light vibration of that sound, is not visible to the human eye. Similarly, when you make light you also make a sound. Action and reaction are equal and opposite; therefore, it operates in reverse. For most of the

Flying Saucer propulsion we use the inaudible sound given off by certain frequencies of light and the invisible light given off by certain sounds. Those are the two main fuels that we use."

Question: "Is the light consumed as other fuel would be?"

Aetherius: "It undergoes a change and the energy created by that change gives propulsion."

Question: "We have been told that there are at least two unknown metals used in the construction of Space-craft. What mechanical and physical properties have they and what is their place in our table of elements?"

Aetherius: "I will refrain from answering that question. If your scientists want to play with titanium it would amuse them and prove interesting. In fact, I understand one of your scientists thinks that the fusing of calcium into it, by very great heat, would produce certain metals which would prove very interesting. Most of the metals we use are amenable to thought and they can be changed, materialised and dematerialised almost at will by the Masters. So therefore, the actual chemical constituents are secret and I do not wish to divulge them."

Question: "There is secrecy to prevent this metal from falling into the hands of Earth scientists?"

Aetherius: "Yes, I may say that this metal has been used upon Earth for thousands of years in ancient Atlantean days and there is nothing new about it at all. It is virtually indestructible and it will not rust. Some of the Flying Saucers you see may be 15,000 years old. Your world has to earn that knowledge."

Question: "From what Planets are the Space-craft now coming to Earth?"

Aetherius: "From Mars and of course Luna which is used as a base and from Venus, Jupiter and Saturn. Some also come from Uranus which is the Great Mother of the System.

"There is such a close liaison among the Planets that these Saucers come from most of them, but certain other Planets use Venus for a jumping off base."

Question: "Do the Space-craft come from Planets outside our Solar System to use Venus as a base?"

Aetherius: "A few have in the past, but they are very few and far between.

"I think the Masters *within* this Planetary System will have to help your little world out of its rut. We do not really want intervention from outside the Planetary System—except from God which is outside and yet within."

Question: "Can you tell us something about the atmospheric environment required by the occupants of the Saucers?"

Aetherius: "There again, we need not be so particular about that as you people on Earth would have to be. You would have to have an atmospheric pressure of 14 lbs. to the square inch: ours could be variable. You see, it depends what state we have to travel in. If we travel in a state of cataleptic trance, the pressure does not matter at all. Again, if we travel in a conscious state, it does not matter because we have certain control over gravity; otherwise we would not be able to make the G turns that we do. Because of years of previous preparation our bodies are more adaptable than yours."

Question: "When you operate within the range of our atmosphere, do you do this in a conscious state?"

Aetherius: "Mostly, yes."

Question: "Within our range of atmosphere, what velocities are used normally and also when making sharp turns around corners?"

Aetherius: "We normally travel about 20 miles per second. We create quite a bit of friction and heat at that velocity, but that is compensated for by various mechanisms that we can bring into operation in order to use the energy produced by that friction."

Question: "Is heat transformed into another type of energy?"

Aetherius: "Yes, we do not waste anything."

Question: "Do you control the waste normally taking place in friction?"

Aetherius: "Yes, if we wish. You see, it is not necessary for us to use Flying Saucers at all. We can come here by other means, but it is necessary that Earth people, before the great outpouring of Light comes should recognise the fact that the Earth is just one inhabited body in the Universe. It is necessary to bring about a certain result. That does not mean that you should say, 'I am a lowly form of life, I have no power'. You should look up into the heavens and say 'There is a person more advanced than I am. I can do what he does'. Naturally as we have control of various forces, so that we can travel between Planet and Planet with a physical body, without any other vehicle, when we do use a vehicle we can mould it to our own requirements exactly. It demands a certain knowledge and a certain Spiritual and evolutionary Ascension in order to be able to do these little things, which of course are quite trivial!"

Question: "What is the temperature of those on Venus who use a physical body?"

Aetherius: "The animals have a temperature which varies between 110 and 150° Fahrenheit; that is to say, we have a 40° variation there."

Question: "Then there will be no ice as we know it on Venus?"

Aetherius: "Not naturally, no."

Question: "How about Mars?"

Aetherius: "Mars is much colder. Temperatures at the equator are about 50° above freezing point. They have quite a bit of ice on Mars, which they can use if they

magnetic attraction ——→ *Move/dissolve clouds*

wish. They have a way of making their own water which is allowed to freeze. Within the ice there are very vital mineral elements which they often use. They make water so that it freezes and collects the radiation from the Sun, then they re-melt it again and use it as water. On Mars they can control the weather so that they have the meteorological conditions which are most in harmony with their needs. They have a Space Station which describes a pre-determined orbit, delicately balanced, within the gravitational pull of the Planet itself and from this they can move clouds by magnetic attraction, or they can dissolve clouds, whichever they wish."

Question: "What would they consider an ideal range of temperature for their needs?"

Aetherius: "From about 35° of frost to 50° above freezing point."

Question: "What means are adopted by the Venusians and Martians when they come into our environment, to adapt themselves and their machines to our temperature, atmospheric pressure and atmospheric constituents?"

Aetherius: "We have certain protective clothing, which has very great properties. The Martians occasionally use a type of breathing apparatus which removes a percentage of oxygen from your atmosphere. Your atmosphere is richer in oxygen than they need. But if they stay in a physical body for only a short time, they can put up with this extra richness in oxygen if they wish. They are experts in breathing, of course and they can use only a small portion of their lungs if necessary.

"Certain of the Martian Masters fabricate a body for themselves and leave their own body elsewhere and inhabit this other body. Or they may remotely control this other body by a system of thought which gives it an animation brought about by the thought of the operator.

You can talk to them—they can sit down and so on and you would not realise that only a percentage of the total consciousness of the Master operating such a body is in that body.

"Now, to those of us who come from Venus, environmental conditions do not matter so much. Those who are Adepts can naturally adapt themselves to all kinds of environmental conditions. Just as your Masters can allow Themselves to be frozen in a block of ice and melt it, so we can come to a cold Planet or to a hot Planet and it makes hardly any difference to us. Changes in temperature and atmospheric conditions do not affect us, but bacteria could affect us if we did not wear clothing which maintains around itself a certain magnetic field which will repel any foreign bacteria."

Question: "Are not bacteria susceptible to thought?"

Aetherius: "Yes, some people can destroy bacteria by thought, but we have to be very careful about doing this because certain bacteria in your atmosphere are essential to you. We, in our physical bodies, could repel all the bacteria around us, but that would be harmful to you. Our suits give off a certain vibratory note which will repel all the bacteria which come very close to us, while leaving those around you. The clothing has been thought into being from the universal supply and has been given that property by those people who thought it into being. In the same way, if we wanted to go down to the depths of the ocean, we would think into being clothing which would have the necessary protective properties. If we wanted to go to the Moon, we would think into being clothing with appropriate properties."

Question: "You speak of various types of light and sound vibrations.

"On Earth, we consider light to be one of many possible forms of electro-magnetic disturbance which can be

EVERYTHING IS VIBRATION — light & sound

propagated either through bodies or through a vacuum. Sound we consider to be a disturbance which can only be propagated through air or gases, but not through a vacuum. When you speak of subtle sounds being generated in space, it is difficult to visualise what is meant."

Aetherius: "There is no such thing as sound alone, there is no such thing as light, alone. There is no such thing as oxygen alone; everything contains so much of everything else, but in its more subtle state. You on Terra have, up to now, been able to isolate the colours of light given off by various sounds, you have made a machine which will give certain sounds and the colours of those sounds. Action and reaction must be equal and opposite, so if you obtain colour from sound, you must also obtain sound from colour. I am informed that you have an organ on Earth which will project the colour of sound frequencies on a screen. We have gone much further than that. If you sit quietly in this room and look over there, you see a green light. If you were sufficiently sensitive and really tuned in, you would also hear a certain note being given off by that light. Our machinery can use this energy."

Question: "Then you must mean by sound something quite different from what we mean by sound?"

Aetherius: "Yes, of course we do. Sound given off by light will travel a little quicker than ordinary sound and it will be inaudible to an ordinary ear. It is only possible for you to hear it if you sensitize yourself."

Question: "Sound as we know it, could not pass from the hot filament in the lamp to the glass, because there is a vacuum there."

Aetherius: "Do not forget that there is a friction caused by the light travelling through the atmosphere and that, in itself, will give a certain sound. Even though the most important part of that light is invisible and travels through the ether; it has its reaction upon the particles of gas, it causes a movement of the molecules. That alone gives sound. If you were to alter the length of the vibrations and make it a blue light, that would give you a slightly different sound. That is one aspect of it; *there are six more aspects of it.*"

Question: "If there is no such thing as oxygen alone, then therefore there is no such thing as a vacuum?"

Aetherius: "There is only God. If you were to make a true vacuum, then that would be the most Sacred, Sacred thing that you could do! It would mean that God had agreed that He would be directly in His Presence, in that particular spot, at that particular time. But I do not mean a personal God. A vacuum is the word AUM, because a vacuum contains all there is to contain. Action and re-action must be equal and opposite and must operate right down through the scale, not only in the mathematics you know, but also in the deeper aspects of metaphysics."

Question: "Would that be the sound known as the Voice of Silence?"

Aetherius: "That is so."

Question: "Can you give us any information about what happened to Jesus between the ages of 12 and 30?"

Aetherius: "He did, of course, leave the Planet several times. He visited Mars, Saturn, His own Planet—Venus and also Jupiter. He also spent some time with certain Initiates and what you would call Masters, in the secret retreats throughout Terra. He went to the retreats in Egypt, the Himalayas, America and in the Andes. As you have no doubt gathered, He did visit England as a boy."

Question: "The Master Jesus stated that He came to Earth to save it from catastrophe. Can you tell us to what the imminent catastrophe was due at that time?"

Aetherius: "To the wrong thought and action of mankind. Exactly as it is now, of course. Only now, it is a little more focused on to one or two major points but at that time it was—well—almost individual."

Question: "Has nuclear power been used on any of the Planets safely or is magnetic power used for heating, lighting and propulsion?"

Aetherius: "Certain Planets, especially outside the Solar System, do use nuclear power and it can be used safely if the motive behind its usage is correct. But we do state now and have stated in the past, that *Terra as a whole is certainly not ready in any way at all to use nuclear energy, not even for so-called peaceful purposes!* Most of the Planets in the Solar System do use a magnetic energy which is caused by the reaction of prepared Solar energies upon crystal formations. Some of these crystals are grown by thought, others are grown in a slower way."

Question: "Eventually then we should be able to use nuclear power before we can use magnetic power?"

Aetherius: "No! The other way round."

Question: "Do we have to abandon all forms of nuclear power?"

Aetherius: "Yes, definitely—beyond all shadow of doubt. Abandon it completely. Start to study magnetic power in its non-dangerous forms. I would ask you to think about that in reference to what I have to say regarding motive. Nuclear energy should not be touched at all by you because on the whole the motives of the Governments of Terra are quite wrong."

Question: "Do certain scientists upon Earth know enough about magnetic energy to be able to work on it, without help from you?"

Aetherius: "No, might I say this. When the vessel is clean enough clean water is poured into it. Some scientists have suffered because this clean water has been poured into a clean vessel. Such is your disgraceful law upon Terra."

Question: "Have you recently given Your messages to the

public through any other medium or have You communicated with Overseas Groups?"

Aetherius: "I HAVE NOT DONE SO!

"This present Mental Channel I am using is the only Mental Channel with the exception of two. One is now living in the Himalayas and the other beneath Mount Shasta. The third Mental Channel I am using is the person you see before you. So I would like this known and I would like to warn other groups who make such claims as to being in communication with me, that they should very, very, carefully question their communicators— *who are obviously pretenders.*

"You know, many discarnate entities from the Etheric Realms pretend to be Planetary Entities and as the time goes on this will happen more and more. It is unfortunate that these Intelligencies should waste valuable micro-units of mental energy to put on this *act!* Because when they are found out, as sooner or later they must be, then nothing they have ever said in the past has any value."

Maldek → previous planet

CHAPTER XIII

THE INITIATION OF EARTH

MARS SECTOR 6

'This is Mars Sector 6, reporting from Satellite No. 3, now in Magnetisation Orbit—Terra, during Magnetisation Period No. 1, Present Phase. Subject: *The Initiation Of Earth*.

"As you know, you Terrestrials were offered sanctuary upon the Planet you call Earth some time after you had destroyed the Planet upon which you lived. All that is left of that Planet, Maldek, is cold, lifeless rock, devoid of atmosphere, the remains of a broken world. You came unto this Planet so that you might have the benefit of further experiences through the Great Teacher—Life. Twice in the past you have brought catastrophe to this Planet.

"Today you stand in the valley of decision!

"During this time, the Goddess known as Terra decided to await Her Cosmic Initiation so that the lifestreams upon Her body, gaining experience, could enjoy that experience unperturbed by outside conditions.

"The Karmic Law states that there is a limit to the suffering of a Great One. The Goddess, Terra, must shortly take Her rightful Place in the Cosmic Scheme of evolution. This will mean a reduction in the intensity of the ionosphere around Terra and a resultant high rise in the potency of Cosmic Rays actually reaching the surface of this Planet. This will mean that only those of sufficient development will be able to withstand this Cosmic bombardment.

145

reduction in ionosphere

"Therefore it is obvious that Terrestrial man must sort the wheat from the involved chaff. This is logic.

"Terrestrial man faces many problems in the interim period. He faces the possibility of war brought about by the scheming few, who have successfully trapped the unthinking majority by their insidious conditioning campaign.

"He faces disease which is now prevalent upon the Planet.

"He faces the direct result of another's greed, another's lust for power, another's wrongful control.

"He faces the direct results of those thermo-nuclear weapons he has already exploded.

"He faces the prospect of freak weather conditions caused mainly by the gross disruption of finely balanced Terrestrial magnetic conditions.

"He faces mutation in future generations brought about by cellular disease caused by the mutated acceleration of cellular division.

"These things do men face this night.

"These things can all be put right by man if he decides, this night, to throw his God-given Energies into the channels of construction, away from the channels of destruction.

"SERVICE and CO-OPERATION are the keynotes which will enable mankind to put right these conditions. Indeed, mankind upon Terra has the greatest opportunities ever offered to any other lifestreams in the whole Solar System at any time since its inception; for man upon Terra has fallen so low that the climb back could be far more glorious than any yet accomplished since the inception of this Solar System.

"If mankind used his skill correctly, he could cure all disease upon Terra by a close study of that science you call Yoga; by a close study of that science you call

cure all disease

chromotherapy; by adherence to that science you call homeopathy. These things would cure disease.

"Mankind could, if he used his skill correctly, bring about total Terrestrial disarmament and employ the present wasted Energies in constructive channels so that fertilization of his rich Earth would dispel starvation from the surface of Terra forever.

"If mankind choose to use the Practice of the Presence given by The Great Aetherius, he could—if he used sufficient Energy—then help to ward off the harmful effects brought about by killer dust such as strontium 90, strontium 89 and radio-active iodine.

"If mankind used his skill in constructive ways, he could gradually dispel ignorance by a close study and complete revision of present educational systems and standards.

"If mankind used his skills correctly, he could, with the sword of Truth, slay the dragons, hate, greed and lust!

"If mankind went into the Silence more often, he could bring unto himself greater Peace, greater Harmony, greater Joy. A greater, more complete, realisation of his vast importance in the Cosmic Scheme of things would be made as clear as the dawn to him.

"Indeed, those Terrestrials who work in these ways are those who will enjoy the Millenium of Peace, the Millenium of Enlightenment, which must come to Terra as She moves through space unto a different plane of existence, as She accepts Her long overdue Cosmic Initiation.

2012

"When She does this, as She will shortly, those not ready will be taken to another Planet and there the great teaching and instruction will go on again. (Note 1).

"Terra, this night, is a very different place in comparison with what She will be in a short time.

"I am making this statement of fact. I am making this statement known unto mankind so that he may, even in this eleventh hour, choose. His choice must be backed up by Service, through co-operated effort, in order to bring Enlightenment to his brothers.

"It is not whether you succeed or fail which counts as much as the Service you give from this night.

"This is a Declaration made by The Supreme Council. Whether you accept or reject this Declaration as being true or false matters not. Truth is. *Whether you believe it or recognise it does not alter this fact.*"

You May Choose

"You may choose. You may choose conditions which will be brought about by yourselves; conditions which will take you into a lower realm, or conditions which will give unto you that hitherto elusive condition you call Utopia.

"Shortly, Terra must take Her Initiation. Before She does this, She will shake from Her back those who are not ready for the conditions to come. It is not necessary for any lifestreams to be shaken from This back. All lifestreams, if they worked hard enough, could go forward into greater things than those which they have brought to the surface of this Earth.

"MEN, YOU MUST CHOOSE!

" *There is not a lifestream upon Terra who can in any way escape having to make this decision.*

"These are the last days of the old order. The New Order for you will be deeper Peace, greater Joy, conditions beyond your wild imaginings! Or—rebirth upon a younger World to relive the terrors of the history you have made upon this Planet.

NEW ORDER

↳ *I am in younger World*

"CHOOSE—and ACT!

"This Transmission came from Mars Sector 6, from Satellite No. 3, now in Magnetisation Orbit—Terra, during Magnetisation Period No. 1, Present Phase.

"This Transmission was an Emergency Declaration unto Terrestrial man, reminding him, even again, of his responsibilities to himself, to the Planet upon which he resides and to the whole Solar System.

"Relate, zero, zero, five."

THIS IS THE LAW

THE MASTER AETHERIUS

"Yes, these days are indeed days of decision for the people of Earth! You know, Terrestrial man likes to live in the belief that he is captain of his own ship through Life and yet when he is reminded that he has set a course designed to tear the bottom from this ship upon the dark rocks, he wishes to hide his face from such a declaration as this. You cannot do so, my friends, any longer.

"Indeed, if ever the prophecies were nigh, that time is now! You cannot rebuke the Law for centuries and then suddenly reap the fruits. How can you walk away from your vineyard, spend your time in idleness then come back and feast yourselves upon its fruits? These fruits will have withered. This is the Law, exact in every detail to every individual.

"Terrestrial position does not protect you from the Great Law of Karma. Whether you be ordinary man or king makes no difference. The Law is above all such position. The very Law to which the Great Perfects of Saturn strictly adhere is the self-same Law which will react upon erring Terrestrials.

"The problems upon your Earth are minor ones

and can be solved if you expend sufficient Energy. Terrestrial man is no longer a child, but an individual. He has chosen individuality. He has chosen freewill.

"You know, you cannot make a Cosmic choice and then run fast and loose with it, for you make it for life after life. You cannot try this thing and that thing and cast them off like worn-out garments. You cannot only accept those statements of Law you want to and reject the others. No, no!"

You Murdered Jesus

All answers given already (

"No Planet is faced with any conditions which are in any way impossible to it. There is not a lifestream upon Terra at this time, no matter what problems face that lifestream, who has one single problem which is not answerable. All the major problems which you face in these days have been answered over and over again throughout the centuries, in different phraseology. There is not one lifestream upon Earth at the moment who has not had direct access to the teachings of either Buddha, Jesus, or Sankaracharya. Not one single individual lifestream!

"Where is your memory? Is it so short that you forget the part that you played, nineteen hundred and sixty of your tiny years ago? Have you involved so much that your memory is as limited as that? Well, whether it be conscious memory or unconscious memory, it is there! You have had opportunity after opportunity. You have not risen to your position.

"Very often, some of you have said, 'Oh well, if only such and such a Space man would land and do this, that and the other!' May I ask you a question. *Would you recognise Him if He did?* If you did recognise Him, would you serve Him—*completely?*

"When the person called Jesus came to this Planet

from Venus, the person called Buddha came to this Planet from Venus, did you recognise them as people bringing the Very Torch of Salvation to you? No! You allowed the Great Buddha to beg his bread.

"*You murdered the Great Jesus . . . !*

"My friends, this is the Truth. It is not a pleasant Truth. But it is Truth. You have had greater opportunity than any other people in this Solar System. You have had more outside intervention upon this Planet than any other people in this Solar System and you have done less about it than any other people in this Solar System . . . !

"You have just been informed that these, indeed, are the last days. Have you any conception of the Being who just spoke to you? (Note 2). In the name of All that is Wonderful, if you had, then you should be willing to serve others in every possible way, because you have been asked to do so by a source which is . . . COSMIC!"

Cosmic Voice—A Holy Work

"My friends, you do not need to bring great suffering upon yourselves. Such things are not necessary, if only you *read* your Holy Works and ACT upon them. Our teachings, which we have given continually over the past few years, are all contained in Holy Works. *These Holy Works are referred to, in Terrestrial language as—Cosmic Voice* (Note 3). Why? Because it is the Voice of the Cosmos!

"In these simple statements of Truth, you can find the answer to all your problems. You may say, 'Oh well, we are only fifty, or two hundred, or three hundred people. What can we do?'

"If three hundred people expended sufficient Energy, those three hundred people could light such a Flame in the country of America that all who came within the illumination of this Flame would be changed by it.

Three hundred: *if*—they expended sufficient Energy. We have told you this before.

"May I be permitted, please, to give you people in the country of America a little advice? If you, on the whole, took far less notice of absurd commercials coming over your television and treated other subjects as being more Sacred than you do, greater, deeper awareness would be the result.

"If you did not treat the handful, the *handful*, of legitimate teachers in your country with such familiarity, treated these with a greater respect, holding a more Sacred approach to the genuine teachings coming from other Planets, greater awareness would be the result.

"But what do you do? You talk glibly about the 'brothers this' and the 'brothers that'. Do you really think, are you deluded so much that you really believe that you are entitled to refer to a Cosmic Being as— Brother? My dear friends, may I remind you that such a reference signifies that you, too, are on a par with such a One. Are you? If you say you are, then may I suggest that you look in the textbook of your language and find out the true meaning of the word—*humility*.

"If you were to open your Holy Works and treat the matter therein as being Sacred Material, Holy Material, a greater appreciation would dawn upon you. A greater discrimination would come to you . . .

"The interference factor here is considerable. I want neone in infinitely variable pattern. I want this designation to the basic variation: neem neem six. Execute immediately."

"Executed."

"Thank you very much. I want emergency beam zero zero five."

"Executed."

"Thank you. I want this screening. I want basic Terrestrial screen neem neem seven two zero."

"Executed."

"What is your opinion?"

"I am satisfied."

"Thank you very much, I will continue" (Note 4).

"Yet, the fakes can come oftimes before you and talk glibly with a silver tongue and what do you do? Lose your discrimination! You lose one of the greatest gifts given to you!"

DISCRIMINATE

"DISCRIMINATE! Treat the Real Teachings as being Sacred Teachings and discrimination will come to you like the dawning of a new day. Then you will be fired with a Spiritual ambition, an ambition which will help you to go forward and help to bring Enlightenment to your brothers—to your brothers upon Earth.

"You people can put conditions right upon your Earth, and then your bodies will become less gross, far more sensitive. Your psychic centres will be opened to such an extent that you will have a greater awareness, a deeper Cosmic appreciation, greater Enlightenment, a greater feeling of Oneness. Then you will be able to take your rightful place in the Cosmic Scheme of things.

"Do you want to go backwards or do you want to go forwards?

"It is a lot easier to go backwards. Just continue bursting your bombs and you will go backwards. Continue with your systems of competition and you will go backwards. Continue with your greed, with your hate, with your jealousy and you are sure to go backwards.

"Come forth into Service and you will go forwards!

"Spend all of your spare time in Service to others and

you will go forwards!

"Read the numerous Messages which have been given to men of Earth from this Source and you will go forwards! (Note 3).

"Act upon these Messages and you will go forwards!

"Take the Holy New Age book, The Twelve Blessings and practise these things and you will go forwards! (Note 5).

"*Practise the Presence* and you will go forwards! (Note 6).

"Breathe deeply the Great Pranic Energies coming from the Sun and let these impregnate deep, deep, down inside of you and you will go forwards, because you will vibrate in a different way." (Note 7).

SERVICE

"Service to an enemy is very difficult is it not? Service to an unknown stranger is very difficult, is it not? Service to a friend is easy. It is not counted in the Great Book, you know.

"Mankind upon Terra has brought these present conditions upon himself. These are the Last Days where he must come out of his present state into the LIGHT. He must use his free will.

"Millions of years ago, the race of people now upon Terra chose to use their freewill. They chose to give up Freedom by the use of their freewill. Meditate upon that. Freewill and Freedom are opposite sides of a magnet—opposite poles. In fact, they are poles apart. You chose this. Now, my friends, you are finding the bitterness of your choice.

"But mark you well this: there is sweetness, too, in this choice—not everlasting sweetness—but a great sweetness in this choice, because you can by the use of this hitherto misused freewill, accomplish mighty things—if you choose.

"I think I will leave that thought with you—CHOOSE —FOR YOUR OWN BENEFITS.

"Might I remind you of this fact: the condition upon your Earth is not an impossible one. Even in the midst of darkness, there is still great Light. Thousands of your numbers are working throughout the world to bring great Light. They are working against tremendous odds and *they are succeeding!* Do not sit back though and allow these ones to go on alone. It is your *help* they need, not your sympathy. If you are worthy of the name, human, you will give them this help in every conceivable way and if enough of you do so, you will do great things! You will prove beyond all shadow of all doubt that you are ready to take the next step onwards into the Great Light which is soon due to come to Terra.

"You will prove it to the Lords of Karma, for They are the Beings who know you. You cannot lie to These. You cannot cheat These. Be as insidious as you may, you cannot fool These. They know. You can prove though, by your thought and action to These, that you be ready for this great Cosmic Initiation which is due to come unto the Planet you now occupy. It cannot, even with all the Divine intervention be kept in abeyance much longer.

"When it comes, the involved ones will be sorted, a little roughly possibly, from those who are obviously ready . . .

Go Forward Into Light

"MAKE YOURSELVES READY AND GO FOR-WARDS INTO GREAT, GREAT LIGHT!

"Draw down the great Powers unto yourselves. Vibrate

with this tremendous Power and Energy and go forwards giving service instead of sympathy. Living your belief instead of just talking about it. Co-operating instead of competing. Then you will not only help yourselves, but help hundreds, aye, maybe even thousands of your Terrestrial brothers.

"Mark ye well, oh men of Terra, what has been said. Act upon it, if you be great enough, wise enough, to do so. When you do this, you will become wise in your greatness!

"Before I vacate Transmission Orbit, I will give you all, the benefit of my Invocation.

"I Invoke the Powers from the Masters of the Sun and Saturn, this very moment.

"May these Powers fall upon the heads of all Terrestrials who are ready to receive them, this very moment, so that they may know that—God dwells silently within them all.

"Thank you very much for your attention and your co-operation and may God Bless you all.

"Good night."

MARS SECTOR 6

"This is Mars Sector 6, reporting from Satellite No. 3. Temperature?"

"One hundred and two."

"Neem six two variant nil nil six. Execute. Divorce. Temperature?"

"Ninety nine."

"Acceptable. Mental variation?"

"Alpha nil nil six, minus two zero."

"This designated Beam: Neone in basic pattern, alpha recharge. Relate. Divorce. Opinion?"

"Alpha radiations, normal."

"Heart?"

"Normal."

"Cellular division?"

"Excited; suggest action."

"Acceptable. Neone in eight two variable. Cellular dispensation, minus two six, minus two five, minus two zero. Static. Divorce. Your opinion?"

"Satisfactory."

"Acceptable." (Note 8).

"This Transmission came from Mars Sector 6, from Satellite No. 3, now in Magnetisation Orbit—Terra, through Primary Terrestrial Mental Channel. (Note 9).

"With the Sanction of Interplanetary Parliament based upon the Planet Saturn.

"With the Sanction and Authority of the SUPREME LORDS OF KARMA.

"This was an Emergency Transmission.

"Divorce   neone.   Divorce   Terrestrial   screening. Divorce beam six eight two."

"Executed."

"All Transmissions now discontinued."

NOTES:

Note 1.

This does not mean that those not ready for the New World will be transported to another Planet by Space Craft, but will go there through the experience called "death", to be Re-incarnated on this younger Planet.

Note 2.

This reference is made to Mars Sector 6.

Note 3.

Reference here is made to *Cosmic Voice* now declared by The Master Aetherius to be a Holy Work. Obtainable from The Aetherius Press.

Note 4.

The last ten lines refer to a conversation between The Master Aetherius and another Planetary Being. Aetherius here, requests a beam of protection because of the tremendous interference which was being caused by the dark forces at this time.

Note 5.

The Twelve Blessings is a book of mystic practices given by The Master Jesus through George King. These constitute an extension of the original teachings of Jesus and as such are regarded as a New Age Bible. Obtainable from The Aetherius Press.

Note 6.

See *"The Practices of Aetherius"* pages 24 to 26 inclusive—published by The Aetherius Press.

Note 7.

See *"Your Higher Self Through Yoga"* by the same Author.

Note 8

Mars Sector 6 here is holding a conversation with the same Being who assisted Aetherius (see Note 4). Mars Sector 6 is asking this Being numerous questions regarding the damage to the mental and physical bodies of George King by the interference of the dark forces during this Transmission. The weaknesses found are put right by Mars Sector 6 who is manipulating a beam of Energy. You will notice that at the end of the Transmission, George King has a temperature of 102 and this was brought down to 99, which was considered to be "Acceptable."

Note 9.

See *Cosmic Voice Volume No.* 1, pages 57 to 70 inclusive for a description of The Third Satellite—published by The Aetherius Press.

AUTHOR'S NOTE

The foregoing Transmissions were delivered on April 7th, 1960 in the American Legion Hall, Detroit U.S.A. at 8.45 p.m. while on the American phase of my World tour.

When I had recovered from the deep self precipitated Yogic Trance necessary for the reception of this Intelligence, scores of people from the large attentive audience besieged me. They all declared that this was the finest metaphysical meeting they had ever attended in their lives and the Transmissions far surpassed anything they had ever heard before.

Here indeed is the wisdom of the Planets. Truths which directly affect every lifestream on Earth.

We would all do well to carefully study the great Truths contained in these Interplanetary Prophecies and thereby prepare ourselves for—The New World!

I can do no better than remind the reader of the advice given by that Shining Cosmic Adept—Mars Sector 6.

"Men—YOU MUST CHOOSE!

"There is not a lifestream upon Terra who can in any way escape having to make this—decision.

"These are the last days of the old order. The New Order for you will be deeper Peace, greater Joy, conditions beyond your wild imaginings. Or, rebirth upon a younger World, to re-live the terrors of the history you have made upon this Planet.

"CHOOSE—and ACT!"

AUTHOR'S CONCLUSION

CHAPTER XIV

FLYING SAUCER OPERATIONS AND CONFIRMATIONS

Not only have the Intelligences from Venus and Mars given of their Masterly Advice and Wisdom in a logical and simple way to help man in his struggle for Enlightenment, but they have proved their identity, scores of times in a very practical way. The following chapter is devoted to a few of the numerous Flying Saucer Operation forecasts given to the public by these Interplanetary Intelligences and the Confirmation of these forecasts.

Hundreds of people from all over the world have seen Flying Saucers on dates which were given previously, operating over the countries mentioned. No longer can these Inter-planetary Contacts be laid at the door of the Author's imagination, for they have PROVED their authenticity beyond all possible doubt. A careful study of this chapter will illustrate this even to the most sceptical minded reader.

Although the object of this book was not to prove that Flying Saucers exist but to give their Spiritual message to Earth, nevertheless hundreds of individuals from all walks of life, who have been acquainted with this phase of the Author's work, have immediately attached themselves to the ranks of the believers. Some, including Scientists, Doctors, Clergymen, have even become extremely active on behalf of the Aetherius Society which was founded by the Author because of the world wide interest, which has been caused. These investigators soon saw, as will most readers of the book, that no other explanation for this phase of activity could

163

be advanced, except that these confirmed Flying Saucer Forecasts were given previously by the Beings who man them.

FLYING SAUCER OPERATIONS

SIGHTING FORECASTS AND CONFIRMATIONS

The following Flying Saucer operational forecasts were given by Intelligences living on the Planets—Mars and Venus. This information was picked up telepathically by the Author in a Yogic Trance before public audiences.

Forecast

"Flying Saucers will be operating on July 7th, 8th and 9th generally over the Antipodes. I feel that the vehicles you call Mother Ships should be seen over Australia and New Zealand during that time".

That forecast was made by the Master Aetherius in the Caxton Hall, London, on June 30th, 1956.

Confirmation

The Sunday Telegraph, Sydney, July 8th, 1956.

"R.A.A.F. IN HUNT FOR 'SAUCER' OVER SYDNEY.

"An R.A.A.F. plane flew over North Sydney yesterday investigate a report of two un-identified objects in the air. The pilot found no explanation for the sighting of the objects. The R.A.A.F., was acting on a report from Mr. Alan Light of Lloyd Avenue, Cremorne. Mr. Light had earlier told *The Sunday Telegraph* that he and other Cremorne residents sighted two unusual objects in the sky. Mr. Light was a radar equipment operator with the R.A.A.F. in World War II.

" 'The objects had a metallic appearance and gave off a bright light,' he said. 'They appeared between noon and 1 p.m. about 2,000 feet up. They were almost stationary. The objects disappeared for about an hour but one reappeared again about 10 past 2. They were not aircraft, nor were they weather balloons, I've seen plenty of them.' "

Forecast

September 3rd, 1956, was given as a day of intense Flying Saucer activity over the Australia and New Zealand areas.

This forecast was made by The Master Aetherius on August 25th at the Caxton Hall, London. The following confirmed story report appeared in "Flying Saucers New Zealand" December Issue.

Confirmation

"SWIFT FLYING CIGAR-SHAPED OBJECT SIGHTED.

"*September 3rd*, 1956. Witnessed by many observers, over a distance of 200 miles, a glowing object flying at a low level crossed Auckland heading north-west at 6.45 p.m. on Monday, September 3rd. The most expert observers so far ascertained, were two Air Force Squadron Leaders, K. B. Smith and O. Staple. The officers were at 500 feet making a landing run into Whenuapai Air Force base when the glowing object crossed their path, disappearing to the north-west as their Hastings aircraft touched down. It was in sight for upwards of a half minute. First taken for a jet, Squadron Leader Smith said that they changed their minds quickly when the object revealed its terrific speed. It had a glowing half crescent shaped light in front and a more separated light trailing to the rear.

'This trailing light seemed to pulsate,' said Squadron Leader Staple. The pilots could not see the shape of the object between the lights. Your editor interviewed both officers, both of whom confirmed the press report and gave additional details. 'The object was travelling a flat horizontal trajectory at an estimated height of 2,000 feet' said the Squadron Leaders.

" 'We have not previously seen anything like it. It did not resemble shooting stars or meteors—we have seen plenty of those'.

"Your editor also interviewed Sergeant T. E. Cook, also of Whenuapai. Sgt. Cook, in company with two others saw the object from their car whilst approaching the city on the new northern outlet highway.

"The object was cylindrical in shape, had a glowing light up front and was trailing a pinkish-blue flame-like light from the rear."

Forecast

On the 25th of August, 1956, at the Caxton Hall, London, The Master Aetherius gave the 17th to the 22nd of September as days of Flying Saucer activities over all areas.

Confirmation

The Daily Telegraph, 21st September, 1956.

"An object, like an outsized star, radiating a brilliant white light was seen from the Hastings area last evening. The sun was still shining. The object was obscured by cloud for about 45 minutes. When the sky cleared it had disappeared, observers told the police. They said it was directly overhead. Two local R.A.F. stations confirmed the reports. Spokesmen were unable to offer an explanation. Mr. H. F. Finch, a principal scientific officer at the Royal Observatory, Hurstmonceaux, said last night, "I watched the object through binoculars at Hailsham. It was probably a meteorological balloon. It was two to three miles up and was drifting slowly in a southerly direction. It appeared as a disc when seen through the binoculars and this is how a balloon appears. It appeared to have a bright band across the centre with bright circular patches on either side'."

Confirmation

Empire News 23rd September, 1956.

"Eight days after they thought they heard Flying Saucers thousands of Lincolnshire folk thought they saw one yesterday. High over Cleethorpes promenade a mystery sphere glittered in the blue sky. 'It looked like a glass globe with something white inside' said an eye-witness. But a Meteorological Office spokesman at Manby R.A.F. Station who studied the object said, 'I don't know what it is. It certainly is not a balloon from here.' Eight days ago a mystery explosion rocked homes in the district."

Confirmation

Sunday Times 23rd September, 1956.

"A Flying Saucer was sighted both visually and by radar over Manby, Lincs., yesterday afternoon. The object was at 54,000 ft. and remained apparently stationary for about an hour, though there was a wind of more than 40 m.p.h. at that height. Meteorologists reported it as having a diameter of 30 ft. Two fighter aircraft were sent up to investigate. When they arrived at the point where the object had been seen they found nothing, nor could it any longer be seen from the ground".

Forecast

Although Mars Sector 6 did not give the exact destination of the landing forecast on the 3rd of August, He did give us all a clue as to its eventual destination:

"The Great Masters of The Andes, the Masters who reside below Mount Shasta, certain Masters from the Himalayan areas of Thibet, certain Masters from the Darjeeling area, will be directly approached upon the dates mentioned by our agents. This will cause a re-orientation to be brought about in the expression of their

Knowledge of the Truth which—in due course will be revealed to the thinking Initiates, when they are ready."

And again from The Master Aetherius on the 25th of August at the Caxton Hall two forthcoming landings were mentioned, namely 17th and 18th of September.

Confirmation

The Evening News, Wednesday, 19th September, 1956, under the Heading "C.A.P.S. Andes Explorers Spot 'Snowman', the following appeared:

". . . A stranger story from another Indian village high up on Mount Macon tells of residents seeing a huge cigar-like 'flying saucer', which landed on a big ledge up in the Andes Mountains. The landing they said, was accompanied by earth rumblings and some land-slides. The 'cigar' remained there a day and a night, then took off into space. At night-time it gave off a phosphorescent glow . . . Reuter."

NOT ONLY DID A LANDING TAKE PLACE IN THE ANDES AS FORECAST, but this was also reported in the press. The Master Aetherius when He spoke of the landing stated: "We know of the press control, but certain plans have been put into operation to break this unjust barrier."

Such an uncanny forecast *should* cause a re-orientation of belief in even the most sceptical mind.

Forecast

The Master Aetherius gave November 10th to 19th, 1956, as very important for Flying Saucer activity over New York, Chicago, North America and Canada.

Confirmation

Flying Saucer Review, Jan.–Feb. 1957 reports: *"U.F.O.'s were being reported almost hourly, night and day, for a period of 25 days from November 8th until December 2nd, over South*

Dakota, North Dakota and Minnesota. This represents the greatest concentration of U.F.O.'s since 1952! The peak day was Friday, November 18th. From early morning until late that night, sightings came in from towns in South Dakota and Minnesota describing objects over those areas."

Forecast

January 15th, 1957 was given as a date of Flying Saucer activity over General London areas at about 7.30 p.m. by Mars Sector 6 at the Caxton Hall on January 12th.

Confirmation

The following confirmatory report appeared in the *Daily Sketch on January 16th.*—

"The riddle of five brilliant saucers of light hovering over Ewell, Surrey, was being probed last night by the Air Ministry. Mrs. Ann Harper, a nurse, said, 'They hovered silently for two minutes, then suddenly gained height and hurtled out of sight'. Air Ministry comment:

'No aircraft were over the area'."

Forecast

On WHIT MONDAY, 1956 Mars Sector 6— reported that magnetic clouds were moving through the atmosphere towards Australia. Soon AFTER this astounding revelation, the whole world was startled by the news release that a gigantic radio-active cloud was dangerously near the Australian coast-line.

Mr. Fred Stone, President of the Australian Flying Saucer Research Society, stated in a personal letter:—

"My heart sorrowed as I read on page 26 of Cosmic Voice the reference to my own dear land. Yet this is but confirmation of what we had received in previous revelations!"

This statement of Mars was soon *proved* to the whole world.

On Sunday, March 17th, 1957, at 11.10 p.m. Mars Sector 6 and Mars Sector 8, Transmitted an appeal to Earth to stop H-Bomb tests. In this message, these highly evolved Intelligences warned of the grave dangers of the proposed hydrogen tests, on the Christmas Islands.

In the words of Mars Sector 6, "This message is being translated into several different languages and we are impressing the minds of certain scientists at this moment, even as this message is being received and translated into English. Whether or not these people take notice of the more subtle types of impression, they are at the moment receiving, is up to them. To do more than this, would be to use a force uncommon to our natures."

(See Cosmic Voice, Special Supplement, Issue No. 10)

Confirmation

On April 13th, 1957, eighteen top German scientists—led by 78 year old Otto Hahn, a pioneer of nuclear fission, said to Chancellor Adenauer: "We refuse to take any part whatsoever in making, testing or firing atomic weapons."

This courageous action was followed some months later by 2,000 top American scientists, who sent a declaration of their refusal to take part in atomic experiments, to President Eisenhower.

Leading scientists in Europe and the British Isles also made their protests against atomic experimentation known publicly. Some did listen and were brave enough to act upon the dictates of their conscience!

Forecast

On Sunday May 19th, 1957, at about midday, during a Power Circle on Leith Hill, Surrey, England, a Transmission was received from Satellite 216 and Mars Sector 8. The Intelligences from Mars gave forecasts of coming Spacecraft over Australia and made the following comments:

"The Satellite 216 is now in orbit 800 miles from Terra. This Satellite will come into closer orbit of your Planet. Your observer teams should be on the alert this evening, if you would see certain of the vehicles released by this Carrier Vessel.

"The radio-activity over Australia is some 25 times that of normal."

This Transmission was heard by 39 witnesses.

Confirmation

"*Flying Saucer Review*" *July/August* carried a leading article on the amazing sightings over Australia, extracts of which appear below:

"THE MOST AUTHENTICATED U.F.O. SIGHTING ON RECORD.

"An unidentified flaming object flew across the State of Victoria, Australia, on the evening of May 19th and was seen by thousands of people. Telephone switchboards at Melbourne's weather bureau, police headquarters, airline and newspaper offices were jammed with calls from 5.45 p.m. until 8.00 p.m. It is estimated that over 23,000 sighting reports of the object came in.

"Times given of its sighting at places hundreds of miles apart suggest its speed at nearly 2,000 miles per hour. Reports describe the object as being silver in colour leaving a white or blue vapour trail in the night sky. Its height was well over 40,000 feet.

"The range superintendent of Woomera Rocket Range, Captain Newman, said there was no connection with Woomera.

"Melbourne Weather Bureau officials saw the vapour

trail and discounted the possibility of a meteorite."

"*Flying Saucer Review*" goes on to say that many airline pilots saw the object. Observers said that it emitted large puffs of vapour at irregular intervals.

"Radio Australia broadcast a long report, nearly 500 words, about this sensational sighting. The B.B.C. considered it of sufficient importance to include it in their 10 p.m. news bulletin on the Light Programme that evening."

The article continues by expressing surprise that this full story did not appear in the London newspapers next morning. "There are no orders not to print anything in peacetime, NO ORDERS. However there are occasions when editors are 'requested' not to write about this or that. No actual order is given. It is just a written request from a certain Government committee. "*Flying Saucer Review*" is aware that such a body exists and knows its name and address.

"It is too much of a coincidence that not one of the London dailies carried the most sensational and widely seen U.F.O. sighting on record.

"Maybe it was considered in 'the national interest' to preserve calm by 'killing' the story."

AUTHOR'S COMMENT

Thousands of miles away from Australia, 39 people listened to a message from the very people who had launched this Flying Saucer, perhaps even as it was skimming over other parts of Australia and the Tasman Sea and Puerto Rico where it was also seen by a Pan American Airways pilot. I am of the firm opinion that this particular vehicle was engaged in clearing away radio activity from over Australia.

Since the August/September Issue of Cosmic Voice (see pages 15 and 16 Issue 11) further confirmatory reports have come in which together PROVE the undoubted authenticity of the source of this Space contact.

SPECIAL NOTE: Since the Master Aetherius and Mars Sector 6 first started to give forecasts of future Flying Saucer activities, literally hundreds of people from different countries have seen these vessels, over the places, on the dates mentioned. Thus has Cosmic Voice the privilege of creating an astounding precedent in the world of Flying Saucer literature. We can truthfully claim that on dozens of occasions, we have been able to publish next week's Flying Saucer news, today. This has caused some of our sceptical readers such a mental reorientation that they have now become active on behalf of The Aetherius Society. Slowly, but as surely as grind the Mills of God, these Interplanetary Communicators are PROVING THEMSELVES to interested open-minded researchers, who have the courage to build their opinions on the framework of greater logic.

THE END.